THE LANCE ARMSTRONG PERFORMANCE PROGRAM

THE TRAINING, STRENGTHENING, AND EATING PLAN BEHIND THE WORLD'S GREATEST CYCLING VICTORY

BY **LANCE ARMSTRONG**

AND

CHRIS CARMICHAEL,
coach to Lance Armstrong and a U.S. Olympic
Committee Coach of the Year,

WITH **PETER JOFFRE NYE**

MJF BOOKS
New York

Published by MJF Books
Fine Communications
322 Eighth Avenue
New York, NY 10001

The Lance Armstrong Performance Program
LC Control Number: 2010929128
ISBN-13: 978-1-60671-034-0
ISBN-10: 1-60671-034-6

NOTICE

The information in this book is meant to supplement, not replace, proper road cycling training. Like any sport involving speed, equipment, balance, and environmental factors, cycling poses some inherent risk. The authors and publisher advise readers to take full responsibility for their safety and know their limits. Before practicing the skills described in this book, be sure that your equipment is well-maintained, and do not take risks beyond your level of experience, aptitude, training, and comfort level.

Contents

Chris and Lance at the 1991 USCF National Championships in Salt Lake City. Chris is the passenger on the motorcycle.

Foreword

I first met Lance Armstrong at the U.S. Olympic Training Center in Colorado Springs in 1990. I had just become the new U.S. Cycling Federation national men's road coach, and Lance was an ambitious, confident 17-year-old. He earned a slot on the USCF junior national team by setting a national age-group record on his way to winning the 1989 junior national time trial championship. Despite this significant accomplishment, Lance really didn't know how to efficiently race his bicycle.

Lance had already established himself as one of the nation's top triathletes, beating stars who were 10 years older and at the top of their game. As a professional triathlete, he had a limited understanding of cycling tactics and of drafting, which was illegal in American triathlons. He also lacked patience. In a 50-mile race, if a group of riders broke away from the peloton (main pack) in the first 10 miles and opened a lead of 40 seconds, he wanted to chase them down, not realizing that waiting and timing were also tactics. Despite his obvious strength and fast recovery, he lacked a good sprint to close and win races. As experienced riders jockeyed for position near the finish, Lance lost places. When the contenders suddenly exploded into their sprints over the final 200 yards, Lance could only watch.

His performances at the individual time trial portions of triathlons drew the attention of the USCF coaching staff in the spring of 1989. At their invitation, Lance came to the U.S. Olympic Training Center in Colorado Springs to try out for the

USCF junior program. He met and competed against other talented young riders, including George Hincapie of New York City, who would ride as Lance's U.S. Postal Service Pro Cycling teammate in the Tour de France; Bobby Julich of Glenwood Springs, Colorado, who would place third overall in the 1998 Tour de France; and another Texas triathlete, Chann McCrae, who would go on to score a fifth-place finish in the 1999 world championship road race in Verona, Italy. All four made the USCF junior national team.

In 1990, I joined the organization as national men's road coach with 17 years of elite-level cycling and coaching experience and was now responsible for developing young riders as well as maintaining the men's elite road program. As a junior rider myself in the late 1970s, I competed as a member of the junior national team with future Tour de France champion Greg LeMond, future Tour of Italy and Tour of Switzerland winner Andy Hampsten, and others who set the standard for the sport in the 1980s. I turned pro in 1985 on the 7-Eleven Cycling Team that went to Europe and blazed a trail for American teams abroad.

When I first met Lance in Colorado Springs, I saw in him the athletic potential that LeMond had radiated. Lance and his teammates also displayed similar athletic talent and the personal drive for excellence that LeMond, Hampsten, and others possessed. Greg LeMond had pushed the bar of performance higher for future generations. I could see that Lance had what it took to do the same.

A frequent problem that coaches encounter is a star athlete who insists on doing things his way. Luckily for me, Lance was never like this. Soon after we met, I took Lance and his teammates shopping for clothes in preparation for a spring racing trip to Italy. Lance readily took my advice about necessary cold-weather gear that he rarely had to wear in his native state of Texas. His attentiveness and appreciation for the advice were both positive signs that we were going to develop a strong relationship.

On another trip, Lance scored a team-best fifth-place finish at a pro-am race in Sweden. More important than his strong finish, the race represented an impressive performance against young professionals who, in only a few weeks, would go on to compete in the Tour de France. Lance possessed a great deal of potential, but I wondered if he was capable of realizing it and performing to that level.

As a young rider, Lance had a hard time pacing his energy on the bike. He took off on his own way too early in races. Sometimes, he would solo and win. Other times, he would get caught near the finish by the peloton, and nearly everyone would roar past him.

Initially, my coaching focused on developing his tactical awareness along with developing his endurance and commitment to cycling and his training. He had the ability and set high ambitions for himself. He just needed focus and experience to meet his goals.

As Lance's coach, I also worked on intangibles, such as how he conducted himself as a leader, both on and off the bike. I knew strong leadership skills would make him attractive to a professional team since many team strategies are built around the strengths of their best riders. Good leadership would help inspire his teammates on our young national team to ride for him and sacrifice their individual glory to help Lance win in competition against the Italians, Russians, and other national teams. I had seen strong riders on pro teams who went above and beyond themselves to support leaders like Greg LeMond, and I knew Lance could inspire the same treatment.

Lance learned to treat his teammates as unique individuals who are irreplaceable. In races where a teammate sacrificed himself to chase down breakaways and keep Lance in contention for the finish, he made sure that he received recognition for his efforts by thanking him both personally and in front of the team. Lance also shared any prize winnings. During the long cycling season, he also rode strategically to support a teammate's victory. Part of being the team leader is gracefully taking the pressure from the press, setting a positive example, often carrying additional team responsibility, and taking the initiative to lead the team when occasions arose. Through his conduct, he would inspire his teammates to excel beyond their own expectations. Both on and off the bike, Lance behaved with grace under intense competitive pressure and media treatment that was often brutal. Later, when Lance joined the Motorola Cycling Team and turned pro after the 1992 Barcelona Olympics, he continued developing those skills under Motorola's team director, Jim Ochowicz. All of these qualities showed as Lance led his U.S. Postal Service team in the 1999 Tour de France.

It took years of hard work for his racing skills and leadership to come together. When I first started coaching Lance, like any novice, he made mistakes, but he turned them into positive learning experiences. Shortly after the start of the 1990 amateur world championships road race in Utsunomiya, Japan, he broke away alone. Lap after lap around the course, he kept pounding away—a really long solo. After he completed a lap, he would spot me standing beside the road, and he would waggle his hand with the pinky finger and thumb extended—the University of Texas Longhorn symbol—a display of his Texan pride.

His solo split up the race. The European riders chased hard and strung out the peloton in a long file with riders constantly dropping off the rear when they couldn't sustain the pace. In the second half of the race, a group of about 20 riders caught him. The winning break emerged from this group, and Lance finished 11th. He scored one of America's best performances in amateur world road race championships since Mark Pringle's 10th place at the 1977 road race in San Cristobal, Venezuela. What was so impressive was that Lance spent considerable energy off the front and still finished 11th. It was clear that he had a huge engine, which was a major asset. If he had conserved his energy better, he could have won a world championship medal. This told me he needed to learn more.

Always a high achiever, Lance constantly pushed to develop his talent while applying what he learned. In 1991, he demonstrated that he was catching on to racing strategically. A breakaway up the road in the early portion of an event didn't agitate him the way it used to. He also had developed a good sprint for the end of races. He improved his climbing ability in the hills. All of those improvements helped him that year to win the Settimana Bergamasca 10-day stage race in northern Italy.

By the spring of 1992, he was flying. He went to Spain as a member of the USCF national team and won two short stage races. When we returned home, he won the Atlanta Grand Prix against the pros. Three weeks later, he again rode to victory against the pros in the Thrift Drug Classic in Pittsburgh.

His performances earned him a contract in 1992 to ride for the Motorola professional cycling team. In 1993, he ignited the sport by winning $1 million after he swept the West Virginia Classic stage race, Pittsburgh's Thrift Drug Classic, and the U.S. national professional road race championship in Philadelphia. The next month, he captured a stage in the Tour de France. He capped the season by winning the World Championship Road Race in Oslo, Norway. All of this when he was still only 21 years old. Lance was starting to realize his potential.

For the next few years, he performed well. His 1996 season got off to a fast start with an impressive spring season in Europe that included victory in Belgium's prestigious Fleche-Wallone and second in the World Cup's Liège-Bastogne-Liège. In May, he won five stages of America's Tour DuPont, and won the overall victory in convincing fashion. In June, however, I started to notice abnormalities in his training. After he won the Tour DuPont, he took 3 weeks off and went back home to Texas—a rare break for Lance. In his training for the Tour of Switzerland in June, he needed a few days of recovery time after each hard day—also unusual for Lance.

He rode the Tour of Switzerland solely as preparation for the Tour de France, yet he wasn't responding with his characteristic snap. In fact, he struggled. The Tour of Switzerland took a lot out of him. I was perplexed. Soon after, he started the 1996 Tour de France. We considered the Tour to be an important preparation to ride in the Atlanta Olympics road race later that summer. In the Tour's first week, rain poured. Lance picked up a respiratory infection and pulled out. At that point, I knew he wasn't going to be a favorite going into the Olympics. At the Olympics, he finished 12th in the road race and 6th in the time trial. Not bad, but below Lance's potential.

Little did I know that cancer was starting to manifest itself that June, when he was riding the Tour of Switzerland. Doctors later determined that he was clearly racing with this malignancy in him during the Olympic Games in late July.

As USCF national coaching director, I had taken the national team in early October to the World Championships in Lugano, Switzerland. Lance's agent, Bill Stapleton, telephoned me from his office in Austin, Texas, with the news that Lance was diagnosed with testicular cancer. I was dumbfounded. He turned the phone over to Lance, who confirmed the news. Lance added that he was going to hold a press conference in Austin to announce that he had cancer and was going to start chemotherapy. A chill went down my spine. I hung up the phone and didn't know what to do or how to deal with this. As his coach, I have to figure out how to make things better. Lance had cancer. I was at a loss about how to handle it.

I wanted to inform the national team members before reporters ambushed them with the news. So I called the national team members together and told them that Lance was going to hold a press conference to announce he had cancer. No one said a word. I remember going back to my room afterward and not sleeping the whole night, wondering where this was going.

Lance's whole chemotherapy treatment period is a dark period for me that I don't like revisiting. It was difficult watching Lance's body deteriorate as he fought for his life. His character during this time didn't deteriorate, however. If anything, it gained strength.

Just when I thought things couldn't get worse, they did. Since the Motorola Corporation contract was expiring at the end of 1996, Lance had signed a 2-year $2.5 million contract, along with Bobby Julich, to ride for the French team Cofidis, whose title sponsor is a French insurance company. Soon after hearing about Lance's cancer, Cofidis canceled his contract.

Lance went through the chemotherapy and recovered from his cancer. In April 1997, he met Kristin Richard and fell madly in love. He told me early in their relationship that he was going to marry her. I felt good, really good, for Lance. He was clearly seeing beyond his illness to a new life.

In September 1997, I accompanied Lance to Interbike, the bicycle industry's major trade show, in Anaheim, California, where he announced that he would return to racing. Every European pro team that Lance's agent contacted had replied by fax: Thanks, but no thanks. They treated him as damaged goods. I could see that rejection was hard on him. A little over a year ago, many of those teams were offering to pay him more than $1 million a year to race. Now, they wouldn't pay almost anything.

Since Lance was out of racing for over a year with his chemotherapy treatment, all of his UCI (Union Cycliste Internationale—the sport's governing body) points had expired. Riders earn these points annually through international competition, and the points are used to rank both rider and team. With no points to offer a team and a cloud of skepticism hanging over the potential of a comeback, Lance didn't have much to negotiate with besides his past performances and sheer desire to race again. Lance had to rely on his good reputation within the racing industry and hope someone would take the leap of faith needed to give him a second chance at professional racing.

He finally secured a contract with the U.S. Postal Service Pro Cycling Team. He rented a home in Santa Barbara, north of Los Angeles, to ride in the coastal mountains and leave the pressures of Austin behind. He trained harder than he had ever trained in the off-season.

His intensive training paid off. In early 1998, he went over to Spain with the USPS team for the Ruta del Sol. He finished 15th, the best he had ever done in that race. I noticed, though, that he wasn't comfortable about his return to cycling. Two weeks later, he started the Paris-Nice race and pulled out on the second day. He told me he was going to quit racing altogether.

I worked with Lance's team of advisors, including his wife, Kristin; his agent, Bill Stapleton; his former team manager from the Motorola Cycling Team, Jim Ochowicz; and his mom, Linda. We discussed things with Lance and got him to commit to one more race—the USPRO national championship in Philadelphia in June. If he was going to go out, he would do it on a positive note.

For that race, we conducted a weeklong training camp in Boone, North Carolina. One of the training days concluded with a climb up Beech Mountain, a 5-mile ride on twisting, narrow roads as a cold rain fell. Lance rode with my former 7-Eleven Professional Cycling teammate Bob Roll while I followed behind in a car.

We hit the Beech Mountain climb after covering 100 miles, about 6 hours into the ride. At the base of the climb, Lance dropped Roll and rode the rest of the way solo. He rode the very pavement where fans had painted his name several years earlier for the Tour DuPont. He rode up the mountain as if he were racing again. I remember leaning out of the car window and yelling encouragement to him.

When we got to the top, I stopped and asked if he wanted a ride to the cabin where we stayed, about 20 miles farther. He said, "No, just give me my rain jacket. I'm going to ride back."

I could see in his eyes and the way he moved that in his mind, Lance had decided to return to racing. Knowing that he could do it, he was going to do it on his terms and no one else's. Sure enough, in his first race back in Europe, the Tour of Luxembourg, he won.

This preparation helped him ride well in the USPRO national championship road race in Philadelphia. In fact, he played a significant role in helping his teammate George Hincapie win.

From there, Lance went on to make his remarkable comeback. Remarkably, within 18 months, Lance returned to the top of professional athletics by winning the 1999 Tour de France—only the second U.S. rider, after Greg LeMond, to win it. Lance had come a long way from an unschooled but talented triathlete to a dedicated international cycling champion.

You may wonder how he did this. It all started with believing in himself. Along with a strong mental focus, he worked hard and followed a proper training program. When Lance returned to competition after his recovery from cancer, he and I examined in great detail what had worked for him in the past—from training rides to eating plans. We made refinements, and with this plan, Lance went on to win the 1999 Tour de France, arguably the world's most grueling athletic event. The core of Lance's training program is what I call the 7-Week Success Plan. This plan has proven highly effective not only for Lance but also for other world-class cyclists such as George Hincapie, Dede Demet-Barry, Bobby Julich, Karen Kurreck, Dylan Casey, and others who are setting the sport's gold standard.

Whether you're a recreational rider, an over-40 masters cyclist seeking fitness and wanting to losing a few pounds, or a competitive cyclist looking for improvement, the same 7-week success plan will help you reach your peak. Now, you can benefit from the same training, mental toughness, strength training, and eating principles and conquer any cycling goal, become a better rider, or simply enjoy the sport more.

Lance has really developed from when we first met 10 years ago. His character and personality have grown deeper. He's a cancer survivor, the founder of the Lance Armstrong Foundation for cancer research, and the father of a young son. True to his form, Lance has proved to be a leader and inspiration for all of us. I'm proud to have been his coach for more than 10 years. As a coach, I've taught him a lot about cycling, and as a person, Lance has taught me a lot about life. Our hope is that you, too, can benefit from his cycling and life experiences.

Chris Carmichael

Lance's victory lap following the 1999 Tour de France.

Introduction

I discovered cycling as a youngster growing up around Dallas. Too young and too small to drive a car, I could still go anywhere I wanted for miles and explore new places on a bicycle. I delighted in the thrill of sharp acceleration downhill, felt the wind in my face, rejoiced at the force on my arms and body from leaning around corners at speed, and thrived on the euphoric sensation that a good workout and honest sweat delivers. I loved riding in the countryside, past fields of bluebells, and smelling the flowers, or the ozone in the air before rain fell. Perhaps the greatest appeal came from exerting control over how fast and where I could go.

As a Texan, I tried playing football, but it wasn't for me. For several years, I swam competitively and ran track and cross-country. From there, it was a short step to competing in triathlons. But what I really loved was cycling, and I quickly connected with bicycle road racing. I liked the sense of friendship and community that comes from riding with others.

Every bicycle racer, from Category 5 entry level and up, dreams of winning the Tour de France. Recreational cyclists have dreams, too, such as completing a challenge ride like a century or the Great Bicycle Ride Across Iowa.

Meeting my coach, Chris Carmichael, in 1990, when I had more ambition than skills, started me on the road to success. He helped me realize my dream of winning the Tour de France.

Chris, who is as wise as a treeful of owls, impressed upon me the value of patience. I had to learn the principles of training, sharpen essential skills (from pedaling more efficiently to shifting and braking), and master techniques such as cornering and sprinting. These all take time to become second nature. How much time? Well, that depends on as many factors as there are individuals. Overall, there is no quick fix. Popular TV infomercials promise great results with 15-minute workouts just three times a week. In reality, it takes commitment and motivation. Throughout the 1990s, except for the year I took off to recover from cancer, I worked full-time at cycling. Yet I had entered the Tour four times between 1993 and 1996, and finished only once. You could say that it took me a decade to win the 3-week 1999 Tour.

Early in my career, many "cycling experts" had typecast me as a 1-day racer. They said I would never win a major multiday race like the Tour de France. My victory supports the belief that anything is possible if you are willing to stick to your dream and keep trying. Realizing a dream, such as mine of winning the Tour, takes patience. Given time and persistent application, we can all improve. That is what Chris told me back in 1990—and he still tells me that today. He says the program is not so much winning as riding better now than before.

Of course, learning how to train and improving my skills have made my cycling safer and more enjoyable. Everything in this book is based on my experiences to help not only elite riders but those who are casual cyclists as well. I still love to go for a spin under the open sky, smell the flowers, hear the birds, and feel the wind on my face. So come on, get your bike and join me for a ride.

Lance Armstrong

The
Promise
of Cycling

1

The Appeal of Two Wheels

In October 1971, shortly after Chris Carmichael celebrated his 11th birthday, he entered his first bicycle race, a 1-mile criterium, near his home in the Miami suburb of Coconut Grove. He finished third and took a trophy home to show his parents. And so began a lifelong devotion to cycling.

Chris distinguished himself by earning a place on the United States Cycling Federation Junior World Team in 1978 with Greg LeMond, a rider Chris's age from Reno, Nevada, whose exceptional talent lit up events wherever he went.

By the time Chris reached his senior year in high school, he knew he wanted to make cycling his life's focus. Even though his parents, both doctors, offered to send him to college, Chris preferred to travel to Belgium, Switzerland, Italy, and wherever cycling took him to test his talents against the best in the sport.

After being selected for the United States team at the 1984 Summer Olympics, Chris accepted an invitation from Jim Ochowicz, general manager of the 7-Eleven Pro Cycling Team, to ride for the new squad in 1985. The team was determined to establish itself in major-league European racing despite facing dim prospects.

Over two seasons of racing in Europe, Chris raised his fitness level to an all-time high. Then, a skiing accident in December

3

1986 shattered his right leg. He endured a long and painful recovery, only to have his fitness wiped out. Ever tenacious, he made up his mind to get back in competitive shape. His form started to come around slowly at first, but by mid-1987, he again scored victories in the United States.

He went back to Europe in 1988 but soon realized that his injury had forced him off his previous top form. Forced to take an exacting look at how races unfolded, his sense of tactics improved. He soon considered coaching, and, in 1990, he joined the USCF as its national men's coach.

Born to Race Bikes

Lance Armstrong was an infant in the Dallas suburb of Plano, Texas, around the time Chris brought home his first trophy. Growing up in Plano, Lance took a different path to cycling.

Initially, his bicycle served as transportation to commute 10 miles across Plano to and from swim practice. He relished working out, especially the exhilaration that comes afterward. In high school, he ran cross-country and track. As he was starting to come of age in the early 1980s, triathlons were introduced. Lance took to them with gusto.

July 21, 1995: Lance, racing with Team Motorola, crosses the finish line to win Stage 18 of the Tour de France. Lance dedicated this win to Fabio Casartelli, who died early in the 1995 Tour.

The Choice of 45 Million Americans

A 1999 survey by the National Sporting Goods Association (NSGA) ranks bicycle riding as sixth among 59 recreation activities among Americans. The survey put bicycle riding after exercise walking, swimming, camping, exercising with equipment, and fishing, and before bowling, basketball, golfing, hiking, inline skating, aerobic exercising, running, baseball, softball, soccer, and tennis. During the year, some 45 million men and women will ride bicycles at least six times.

Who are these 45 million Americans who ride? The NSGA says that most—53 percent—are men. While women make up 47 percent of bicycle riders, the NSGA's survey indicates a significant upward trend among women participating across the entire sports spectrum, including bicycle riding.

The National Center for Bicycling and Walking, a nonprofit clearinghouse for cycling and walking information headquartered in Washington, D.C., estimates that 53 percent of cyclists are adults age 16 and up, and 47 percent are children. According to a Gallup Organization poll, most adults who ride bicycles have college degrees and come from middle-income groups.

Only about 200,000 cyclists actually compete in races. The majority of riders use cycling as a low-key form of recreation that offers exercise to lose weight and maintain a fit and healthy body.

The National Bicycle Dealers Association (NBDA) reports that consumers buy bicycles, components, cycling apparel, books and videos, related merchandise, and services that ring up annual sales of $6 billion. That supports some 2,000 companies that manufacture and sell bicycle-related products.

In the late 1990s, Americans bought more than 11 million bicycles annually. Most were purchased from 6,800 independent specialty bicycle dealers nationwide. Nearly all of those dealers—85 percent—are family-owned, single-location shops, according to the NBDA.

The Discovery Team celebrates its team time trial win of Stage 3 in the 2005 Tour de France.

Triathlons combined his favorite activities of swimming, cycling, and running. He became addicted to passing people and winning triathlons. The better he did, the more he threw himself into training.

His mother, Linda, a single parent, encouraged him to make the most of his athletic talents. With her support and his growing confidence and reputation, he competed from Bermuda to San Diego.

At the same time, Greg LeMond was showing what an American could achieve in cycling, which had long been identified as a European domain. His 1983 World Professional Road Race Championship garnered little attention in the U.S. media. Yet his victory in the 1986 Tour de France caused a sensation. His 1989 and 1990 Tour triumphs thrust bicycle racing into the American cultural mainstream. LeMond gave bicycle racing a unique appeal for ambitious and talented American athletes.

By the time Lance was a high school senior, his reputation as a triathlete and his performances in bicycle time trials generated an invitation from the USCF to visit Colorado Springs in the spring of 1989 to try out for the junior national team. Seizing the opportunity, he rode his way onto the junior national team. Like Chris had done 10 years earlier, Lance decided to pass up college for full-time cycling.

Lance faced the obstacle of developing cycling skills to match his formidable strength and endurance. Chris arrived in 1990 and became the coach who oversaw Lance's development. Lance put his imprint on the sport in 1993 when he won the USPRO national road championship in Philadelphia, a stage in the Tour de France, and the World Professional Road Racing Championship in Oslo, Norway.

In October 1996, Lance stunned the international cycling community with the announcement that he had advanced testicular cancer. He promptly underwent three surgical operations and endured 10 weeks of excruciating chemotherapy. Gradually, he recovered and began to get back into cycling. He realized he

A Ride to Benefit Cancer Research

While recovering from cancer, Lance founded the Ride for the Roses, which is held every April in his hometown of Austin, Texas. Each spring, he flies back home to lead the weekend activities and fund-raising ride that benefits the Lance Armstrong Foundation's fight against urological cancers. The multiday event starts on a Friday evening with a dinner and silent auction, which draws more than 1,000 patrons and includes headliners such as Tour de France champions Greg LeMond, Miguel Indurain, and Eddy Merckx, and Olympic champions Eric Heiden and Bonnie Blair.

On Saturday evening, a program of USCF-sanctioned races for hundreds of the country's fastest men and women cyclists draws large crowds to Austin's famed Sixth Street to watch racers compete around a downtown circuit. All of these activities lead up to Sunday's Ride for the Roses, which has raised millions for cancer research grants.

Get Involved

For more information on how to become active with cycling organizations, contact:

USA Cycling
One Olympic Plaza
Colorado Springs, CO 80909
Telephone: (719) 866-4581
www.usacycling.org

USA Cycling is the governing body for the following organizations.

U.S. Cycling Federation (USCF), which sanctions amateur and professional road and track racing.

National Off-Road Bicycle Association (NORBA), which sanctions mountain bike riding.

National Collegiate Cycling Association (NCCA), which sanctions collegiate cycling.

National Bicycle League (NBL), which sanctions BMX racing.

---

still had a compelling passion for the sport. This time, with Chris still as his coach, he took a new approach to training and racing.

The Lance Armstrong Performance Program

The program that Chris refined with Lance is what led to his astounding victory in the 1999 Tour de France, which reverberated as one of the most dramatic comebacks in sports history. Each day for 3 weeks in July 1999, he held the world spellbound. During the 2,290-mile marathon on wheels, the most grueling and unforgiving of all sports events, he rode with panache. He won all three individual time trials plus an Alpine mountain stage, responded coolly to numerous challenges, and decisively won the Tour de France.

The attention showered on Lance reflected well on Chris, who had left USA Cycling at the end of 1997, but continued to coach

Lance. Two years later, he founded his own business, Carmichael Training Systems (CTS). Carmichael Training Systems offers personal coaching to Lance, other men and women racers, and ordinary riders seeking to make the best of their abilities and time.

Success in all endurance cycling events—road, mountain, or track—requires a well-developed aerobic system. And so the key to the program developed by Chris for Lance is to maximize the body's ability to absorb, deliver, and transport oxygen. The real attraction of the program is that, with a foundation of fitness, you can cycle to a peak performance after 7 weeks of focused training.

The program focuses on reaching fitness goals by training your physical and mental abilities to their fullest. But physical training can provide only half of what is needed to reach peak fitness. Confidence and commitment provide the remainder of what it will take to make you truly ready for a top performance.

A focused training program that combines fitness, technique, and mental preparation will produce peak performances. These principles apply not only to world-class athletes but to anyone who truly desires improvement.

Lance approaching the Stage 10 finish line of the 1999 Tour de France.

2

Cycling Equipment

Perhaps the biggest change in the professional peloton between Chris's career and Lance's is in the variety of materials used to make frames and the shapes of the frame tubes. Some traditionalists remain with steel, which dominated the pro ranks when Chris raced, but more pros, like Lance, have switched to carbon fiber.

Carbon fiber

Lance looks for a frame that is stiff and light yet absorbs road shock to make his 6 hours a day in the saddle more comfortable. He finds what he wants in frames made of carbon fiber. It's also the material of choice in jet fighters, the space shuttle heat shield, and Formula One car bodies. Lance's bicycle has a stock production frame made by Trek. The frame weighs a mere 2.44 pounds, with a carbon fiber fork weighing a little more than 1 pound. Completely built up and ready for the road, Lance's bicycle registers at a featherweight 17 pounds.

Because carbon fiber's qualities give you a light weight without sacrificing strength and stiffness to absorb vibrations, the trend among high-quality frame builders of any material has been to use carbon fiber for all forks. An appealing quality of carbon fiber is that it's stiffer laterally (side-to-side) than it is vertically. The frame doesn't flex under hard pedaling, but it still retains some cushion to absorb road chatter—something that aluminum doesn't do.

Pros: Carbon fiber is four times stronger than high-tensile steel for the same weight and is also rustproof.

Cons: Carbon fiber frames are among the most expensive. They're also difficult to repair, although Trek backs each carbon fiber frame with a lifetime guarantee.

Titanium

Another crossover from high-speed aircraft and spacecraft to bicycle manufacturers is titanium.

Pros: It absorbs road shock to give a comfortable ride, it's light and stiff, and it's also rustproof.

Cons: Titanium is the market's most expensive frame material. A titanium frame with a carbon fiber fork typically costs more than other racing bicycles completely built up and ready to ride, and is difficult to repair.

Steel

Improved steel such as Reynolds 831, Columbus, and Dedaccai are lighter and stronger than ever. New construction techniques with tapered and oval-shaped tubes made of alloys such as chrome-moly, scandium, vanadium, and boron have added tensile strength and surface hardness to further reduce frame weight to less than 3 pounds. This puts the expensive, high-end steel frames to within ounces of carbon fiber and titanium frames.

Pros: With chrome trim and fancy enamel coating, road steel frames take on the quality of jewelry. A well-made steel frame should last many years—nearly as long as titanium and carbon fiber. Steel provides a smooth ride and is easily repaired.

Cons: Steel is subject to rust; spraying an antirust solution into the frame may help prevent it. Inexpensive steel frames, lacking alloys or high-quality tubing such as Reynolds, Columbus, or Dedaccai, are the heaviest on the market.

Aluminum

Aluminum is widely considered the best buy for entry- and midlevel bicycle frames. The late 1990s saw a big surge in popularity of aluminum frames in some pro teams.

Pros: Aluminum is reasonably priced. It's lightweight and rigid, and also rustproof.

Cons: It doesn't absorb shock like steel, titanium, or carbon fiber, and is subject to metal fatigue. Its estimated life expectancy is approximately 5 years. It's difficult to repair.

The Right Fit

To make sure that a road bicycle fits properly, insist that the bicycle shop personnel do a proper fitting before you purchase a bike. The simple procedure involves measuring your inseam, arm length, distance across your shoulders, your foot, and your torso. These measurements are used to determine the size of the frame as well as the bicycle's handlebar, stem, and pedals. The object is to give you the right fit so your bicycle feels comfortable and maneuvers easily.

Take the bicycle out for a brief ride to get its feel. Try the brakes, make turns, and get a feel for how the bike maneuvers. Run through the gears, which should function smoothly and quietly. Have the shop's mechanic make adjustments if something isn't right, and go back out for another ride.

Specialty Bikes

Bicycling has seen a rising popularity in bikes other than the traditional road or mountain bikes. Here are two of the most popular.

Tandem

Bicycles built for two allow couples with different strengths to exercise together while still being close enough to talk. In the division of labor, the rider who sits in front is called the captain. He does the steering, applies the brakes, and shifts the gears. Behind is the stoker, who adds pedaling power.

Tandems are especially good to ride in a headwind. When a tandem team rides alongside a couple of regular bicycle riders and everyone exerts the same effort, the tandem team will pull away quickly. Tandems make great pacers for a cyclist seeking to train faster.

Recumbent

Sit back and enjoy the ride! Recumbents derive their name from your position on the bike—sitting in a reclining position, legs and feet in front, and steering with your hands. Some recumbents feature a sophisticated chain-drive system to allow two cyclists to pedal back to back. Because they are placed closer to the ground, recumbents allow for greater speed. Even more important to most recumbent riders is the comfort. There's none of the saddle soreness or numbness that can occur on what recumbent riders call wedgie bikes—standard road bikes. Recumbent bikes are good for people who have back problems that prevent them from riding traditional bikes.

Components

Integrated shift/brake levers

Lance joined the USCF national team when integrated shift/brake levers were introduced as an alternative to the traditional down tube shifters. These new levers meant that he could keep both hands on the handlebar for shifting. The system allows shifting and braking downhill around corners. That helps him always pedal in the right gear.

Bruce Galloway, marketing and promotions manager at Shimano, which introduced the integrated shifting/braking system, explains that the idea behind the new system was to improve control of the bicycle. "The system helped to make cycling safer and to make shifting easier and quicker," he says.

Handlebars

In the 1990s, standard drop handlebars gained an ergonomic design that features a straight section in the handlebar's second curve. The straight ergo grip permits you to rest your hands comfortably and gives easy access to the integrated shift/brake levers. There are aftermarket products that allow you to turn your standard bar into an ergo bar—usually an insert that is placed underneath the handlebar tape.

As scientific as the new handlebar design may be, Lance prefers the traditional standard curved drop handlebar because he finds it more comfortable.

Headsets

Traditional headsets involve one or two locknuts that secure the headset to the frame where the steerer tube at the top of the fork goes up the inside of the frame head. Adjusting the locknuts requires practice to get the knack of tightening them snugly without freezing the handlebar. In the late 1990s, a new kind of headset came out of mountain biking that made locknuts lighter and easier to adjust.

The traditional steerer tube's threaded head involves a cone and top nut that tighten against one another. From innovative mountain bike designers came threadless headsets. The parts simply slide onto the fork instead of screwing onto the threaded steerer tube. The threadless handlebar stem clamps onto the steerer tube with an Allen wrench that locks it securely enough that no amount of abuse will alter it. Lance, a traditionalist in road bike components, decided to go threadless in 2000.

Saddles

How the saddle is shaped is more critical for riding comfort than the amount of gel or foam padding. In the mid-1990s, bicycle saddles went through many alterations in design. Here are some of the changes introduced by manufacturers.

★ Widely flared back portions, which better reduces pressure on sensitive areas and supports the "sit" bones (ischial tuberosities)

★ Hollowed-out centers, which address complaints that both men and women have of saddles causing discomfort to their crotches

★ Shallow grooves along the length of the saddle that both widen toward the rear and split the saddle into a Y to reduce pressure on the rider's anatomy

★ Oval-shaped gel padding running lengthwise in the center and the nose for added softness

Georgena Terry, of Terry Precision Bicycles in Macedon, New York, helped lead the way in manufacturing wider saddles specifically for women. She also patented the hollowed-out saddle center.

Saddle shapes and padding also are a matter of individual preference. Lance, like other competitive cyclists, rides a lightly padded racing saddle because his weight is evenly distributed on the saddle, handlebar, and pedals. He also wants minimum padding to avoid bouncing in the saddle, which is an energy-wasting motion.

Pedals and Shoes

Lance's 1999 Tour de France victory marked the fastest ever of the 86 Tours, averaging more than 25 mph for 2,290 miles. Many factors contributed to his Tour speed record. One was the clipless pedal and shoe system that features a stiff sole and firm connection to the pedal. This combination enables Lance to efficiently deliver leg power to the pedals. Styled after ski bindings, the sole of the shoe attaches to the pedal with a cleat that snaps firmly into place, yet releases with a twist of the ankle.

Lance (and nearly everybody riding competitively today on both road and mountain bikes) has a clipless pedal system. The tight fit of the shoe to the pedal is why Lance prefers clipless pedals to the toeclips and straps that prevailed for some 8 decades, until the mid-1980s. Pedals make for important balance points for cornering hard, descending with stability, and accommodating all of the shifts in position that take place in the saddle during the course of the ride.

The drawback of clipless pedals is that the cleat connecting the sole to the pedal protrudes, which makes walking awkward.

Lance prefers the standard pedal rather than a smaller one because he wants a solid base under his feet. He also likes the "float" feature of clipless pedals that allow his foot to swivel a few degrees in either direction on the pedal to give his knee a rest in the pedal stroke. Floating clipless pedals are the preferred pedal of many riders, in contrast to the fixed pedal that doesn't allow movement.

"Clipless pedals changed cycling shoes a lot because the shoe

Saddle Discomfort
Affects Both Men and Women

Andrew Pruitt, Ed.D., who has headed the sports medicine program for the U.S. Cycling Federation and currently directs the Boulder Center for Sports Medicine, finds that saddle discomfort is evenly divided among men and women in his practice.

"It's more common than we previously thought, but it's not epidemic," says Dr. Pruitt. "Most of the complaints involve soft-tissue discomfort such as skin, fat, and muscle, rather than nerve impingement of any kind in an artery or vein. The problem is not just unique to men, who complain of penile numbness. Women also suffer labial bruising and chafing. A chief reason is that the pelvis was never meant to be weight-bearing."

Here are some ways to prevent saddle discomfort.

- Make sure the saddle is level and raised to the proper height (for more information on proper height, see Riding Position on page 35). "If the nose is tipped up, then the rider is sitting on a log splitter," Dr. Pruitt warns. "After the saddle is set

had to be better made," explains Sandy Nicholls, marketing director for Giordana Clothing in Charlotte, North Carolina. "The opening where the foot enters the shoe is smaller than that of a shoe made for a toeclip and strap. The opening has to be smaller because the shoe holds the foot in place during all the strain on the pedal. The integrity of shoes increased a great deal."

Clipless shoes are offered in nylon or carbon fiber soles, with carbon fiber being found on the more expensive shoes. Fresh out of the box, the nylon sole and the carbon fiber sole may feel equally stiff. But the properties of carbon fiber, the same material in Lance's frame, make for enduring stiffness. "A year down the road, the carbon fiber sole will keep its stiffness but the nylon sole won't," Nicholls says.

level, make sure to check it from time to time in case a bolt loosens and the nose creeps up."

- Don't tolerate discomfort or pain. At the first symptom, and if the saddle is level and height is proper, then try lowering or raising the saddle or shifting its fore and aft position.

- Change position on the saddle to let the blood flow through. Slide forward or back on the saddle along straight roads. Shift slightly sideways around corners and downhill bends.

- Check the handlebar height in relation to the saddle. "Most people forget about how the height of the handlebar determines how they sit in the saddle," Dr. Pruitt observes. "A guy who is too tight to bend over at the waist and touch his feet with the tips of his fingers may be at risk for saddle discomfort. By raising his handlebar to the height of his saddle, he will relieve pressure on his crotch."

- When riding a stationary trainer, get off the saddle every 5 minutes or so to relieve pressure on the crotch.

Velcro and mechanical closures took over from laces in the early 1990s because they make straps easy to adjust while on the fly. Laces don't offer that option. Today, the combination of one or two straps with a Velcro closure and a mechanical closure system has become de rigueur on cycling shoes. It secures your foot firmly in the shoe without subsequent loosening, which eliminates a problem common to laces. After several years of use, Velcro will wear out. By that time, however, you're usually ready to buy a new pair of shoes.

Accessories
Helmets

Lance wears a helmet on all his rides. The only exception he makes for wearing a helmet is during a few Tour de France stages that go up the mountains. He rides bareheaded then to stay as cool as possible. Otherwise, he has a helmet on his head.

Hard-shell bicycle helmets like the one Lance wears have proliferated because they are light (as little as 9 ounces), have many slits for ventilation, offer good protection, and are reasonably priced.

Helmets are made with expanded polystyrene, a stiffer version of the white picnic-cooler foam. Tests show that upon impact, the expanded polystyrene spreads out the length of the impact to soften the blow of striking the pavement.

There is a history behind helmet standard certification. Two separate organizations had issued bicycle helmet performance standard certification stickers. One was the blue certification sticker of the Snell Memorial Foundation in St. James, New York. The other was the lime green sticker of the American National Standards Institute in New York City. Both organizations conducted tests separately to make sure products met safety standards. As Tom Larter,

product manager at Giro Helmets, based in Santa Cruz, California, points out, two separate organizations issuing certification standards caused confusion. In May 1999, the federal Consumer Product Safety Commission standard went into effect and took over as the certification standard for bicycle helmets, explains Larter.

Lance Armstrong wearing an aerodynamic helmet in a time trial.

Listen to the **COACH**

Tired of standing beside the road and pumping and pumping? CO_2 gas cartridges inflate a tube in 5 seconds. They're small and light enough to fit conveniently in a jersey pocket. The biggest advantage is the speed of inflating a tire. A chief disadvantage is that if you don't fit the adapter properly on the valve for a tight seal, half or more of the gas could rapidly leak out. You get no second chance with a gas cartridge, which will inflate one tire. For that reason, it's best to carry at least two or three cartridges.

What's the difference between a $30 helmet and an expensive one? "What the customer is paying for are more features, particularly the number and size of vents for the air to flow through," Larter says. "What a customer should look for is a helmet with vents that run air in the front, over the top of the head, and out the back."

As you would do with any piece of apparel, try on the helmet to make sure it fits. Adjustable straps in the helmet will help it fit so that it sits level and comfortably on your head. Examine the chin buckle for long-term durability. Buckles are made to snap in place and to release in a simple yet efficient manner. Have a friend try to pull it off gently from the front and back. If the helmet stays on, it passes the test and likely will protect you in a crash.

High temperatures (hotter than 100°F) will melt any hard-shell helmet. It shouldn't be left in your car or garage, or near direct or indirect heat. To clean your helmet, wash it with mild soap and water.

Replace any helmet after a crash. Some manufacturers, such as Giro and Bell, offer replacement policies too good to refuse. Otherwise, manufacturers recommend replacing your helmet every 5 years.

Computers and Heart Rate Monitors

Handlebar computers and heart rate monitors provide Lance with precise information that eliminates guesswork. Computers offer accurate information on current speed, maximum speed of the ride, trip distance, and total distance. Lance's heart rate monitor tells him how hard he is working. Lance feels that they are indispensable to his training and creates his workouts based on heart rates.

Pumps

Since Lance first started riding as a triathlete, he has always kept two kinds of pumps. One is a floor pump in his garage that he uses to inflate his tires before going on a ride. The other is a frame pump that he carries for fixing a flat tire on a ride.

For a floor pump, look for one that delivers the maximum amount of volume per stroke. Check to see if the manufacturer offers a lifetime warranty.

Frame pumps come in sizes ranging from minipumps as small as 6 inches (convenient to fit in a jersey pocket) to the length of a top tube. Minipumps need a lot of strokes.

Road bike pumps have a narrow barrel, about 1 inch in diameter, to inflate tires to high pressure, from 100 to 120 pounds per square inch. Check to see if the manufacturer offers a lifetime warranty.

Mountain bike pumps have a slightly larger diameter barrel to move a greater volume of air. Mountain bike tires run on low pressure—45 to 50 pounds per square inch to inflate a tire of 2 inches to 2¼ inches for a softer off-road ride. Check to see if the manufacturer offers a lifetime warranty.

Clothing

High-performance fabrics for jerseys, shorts, and gloves offer better fit and greater comfort than cotton or wool. Leading manufacturers use the latest technology to construct clothing that is lighter in weight, less bulky, and easier to care for than cotton or wool. Cotton T-shirts are all right to wear on a summer afternoon, but Lance wouldn't even consider wearing one on a ride. Tucked into shorts, a cotton T-shirt billows like a sail and produces drag. Cotton's chief liability is that it soaks up moisture and retains it.

"High-performance fabrics like Lycra transfer moisture away from the body, up through the fabric, and outside to evaporate so that the garment stays drier and the rider remains more comfortable," explains Giordana Clothing's Nicholls.

Jerseys

Jerseys come with a choice of 4-inch neck zippers or 14-inch zippers. Lance prefers 14-inch zippers so he can open the jersey front for greater cooling when riding uphill or in the heat. Jerseys come with three rear pockets, which are handy for carrying a wallet with money and identification, keys, handkerchief, and snacks. High-tech fabrics are preferred because they are lighter than cotton and wool and hold their shape better.

Shorts

Chris started competing in the era of black wool cycling shorts, which had worked well for generations of riders. But he wouldn't go back to wearing them since high-performance fabrics were introduced in the early 1980s. Cycling shorts, which are designed to be worn without underwear, have a soft liner in the crotch that doesn't bunch up the way cotton or nylon running shorts to do on a saddle. New liners feature antibacterial chemicals to reduce the risk of developing saddle sores. The antibacterial treatment lasts from 50 to 100 washings, Nicholls says.

Lycra cycling shorts, however comfortable they may be for Lance or Chris, don't appeal to everyone because they don't hide anything. Clothing manufacturers such as Giordana and Nike also make baggy cycling shorts made of other lightweight fabrics with a form-fitted liner. Baggy shorts are popular among mountain bikers and tourists who get off their bicycles to explore shops. Baggy shorts feature side pockets, which cycling shorts traditionally lack in the quest for a more aerodynamic ride.

Gloves

Lance wants little padding on his palms. He uses gloves to wipe his tires clean when he rolls through gravel or over a section of pavement containing broken glass. For time trials, he wears smooth Lycra gloves to help him slip through the air.

Recreational riders may prefer thick gel gloves that absorb

road vibrations through the handlebar. Another popular feature on gloves is a terry cloth portion from the forefinger to the thumb for wiping a sweaty brow or runny nose.

Rain Jackets

You never know when rain or cold weather might strike when you are out on a long ride, so it is always smart to pack a rain jacket. Cycling rain jackets, or capes, are made of nylon and Gore-Tex or other breathable synthetic fabrics that are water-resistant and so compact when folded, they fit into the rear pocket of any cycling jersey. They're great if you need an extra layer of protection while cycling in wind or rain. Lance takes advantage of his jersey's rear pockets to carry a folded nylon jacket.

Stationary Trainers

Stationary trainers are every dedicated cyclist's best friend. Lance uses them for many purposes—to train indoors during foul weather, to make adjustments to his riding position, and for pre-race warmups. Stationary trainers offer turbo fan resistance with a lightweight aluminum fan as well as magnetic resistance with five levels. They fold flat for storage, which makes them convenient to pack with a bicycle for warming up before an event. Here's what you should look for when shopping for a stationary trainer.

★ The more expensive it is, the stronger the trainer's metal frame supporting the bicycle will be, and the more features are included, such as an adjustable resistance unit.

★ Make sure that the stationary trainer fits the rear wheel of the bicycle that you will use on the trainer. Most trainers are built to accommodate a standard 700C road wheel (the European equivalent of a 27-inch diameter wheel) in the mounting cones where the rear wheel attaches to the trainer. Some triathletes and smaller women cyclists ride a 650C wheel that may not fit in the standard trainer's rear-wheel holder, so be sure to check.

Lance takes his stationary trainer to races to warm up before a time trial. Riding on a stationary trainer controls his environment, which leaves him free to concentrate on warming up properly.

3

Essential Maintenance and Repair

The bicycle is an amazing piece of technology when properly maintained. But like any machine, from time to time every bike is going to need some attention.

A new bicycle should be taken to a bicycle shop for a postpurchase 30-day check. Most shops offer a free tune-up as part of a new bicycle's 30-day break-in period. Under your weight, spokes loosen, making the wheels wobble; derailleur cables stretch, making gear changes awkward; and bolts that attach crankarms and other parts loosen. These changes can make a dream bicycle perform like a lemon. In fact, your components are only settling in for the long haul and just need a little touch-up. After a 30-day tune-up, the variety of parts that make up a bicycle ordinarily fit securely.

Before and After Each Ride

It's well worth your time to do a pre- and postride check on your equipment. The vast majority of potential problems will be discovered this way. You'll end up saving money and wear and tear on your bike, and you'll prevent potential crashes. These checks should take no more than 15 minutes. If you've kept your bicycle in good shape, you may need to spend only 5 minutes.

Check the tires and wheels. Make sure your tires are in good condition. Make sure that they are not worn to the point that the tube is starting to poke through the tire sidewall or tread. Look for any developing bubble, especially along the sidewall casing, and replace the tube promptly, because sooner or later it will cause a blowout. If you have tubular tires, as Lance does, check the condition of the glue holding the tires to the rim. Check that both wheels are centered in the frame and that the wheels are fastened securely.

Inspect the brakes. Squeeze the brake levers to make sure that they have adequate travel without pressing against the handlebar. Over time, the cables stretch and the brake blocks wear down, which affects how much room the levers need to close the brakes. Turning the barrels on the brake calipers or brake

Bicycle Tool Kit

To handle quick repairs on the road, carry a small tool bag behind your saddle. It should contain the following items.

- Spare tube
- Tube patch kit (contains patches, glue, and sandpaper; check the glue frequently since it tends to dry out once opened)
- Tire patches (homemade 1- by 2-inch pieces of denim or canvas used to cover tire cuts)
- Tire levers
- All-in-one minitool such as the Cool Tool (a small tool that includes 4-, 5-, 6-, and 8-mm Allen wrenches; chain tool; screwdriver; spoke wrench; adjustable wrench; and more)
- Frame pump, set to fit your valve type
- Small section of wire (handy for fixing broken things)
- Emergency money
- Identification (write this information inside your helmet, too)

Correct placement and fit of rear brake pad.

levers is often all you need to do to take up the slack. Worn brake blocks should be replaced right away.

Inspect the front and rear brake pads to make sure they fit squarely on the rim surface. Sometimes, brake pads slip and rub against the tire sidewall, so they need to be adjusted. Also, both front and rear brake cables should respond lightly and smoothly to the touch and snap back when released. Any drag indicates that the cables need to be greased.

Test the frame. Make sure the handlebar stem is firmly in the frame fork by holding the front wheel between your knees and gripping the ends of the handlebar to give it a gentle shake. If the handlebar holds, it's all set. If it gives, the stem needs to be tightened. (This applies more to threaded headsets.)

Test your seat. Grab the saddle to check that it's secured tightly to the seatpost. It's a good idea to inspect the seat and saddle bolts once a month.

Check links, nuts, and bolts. Make sure the chain is lubricated so that the links all move easily over the sprockets without skipping.

Check nuts and bolts of all accessories such as the cyclecomputer, water bottle cages, and any racks on touring bicycles. Bounce the bike to listen for any rattling, which is an indication of loose parts.

Once you're back home, take a few minutes to service your bicycle with these simple steps.

★ Check the tires and brush off any foreign matter on the tread and sidewalls.

★ Clean debris from the rear sprockets and front chain-rings.

★ Dry off a wet saddle.

★ Wipe off a wet chain with a rag and lubricate lightly. If the chain is clogged with sludge, wipe it down with some solvent on a rag.

Routine Maintenance

To keep your bicycle in top condition, do the following things every month, or more often if you're riding more than 4 days a week.

★ Wipe down the entire bike with a damp rag, except near bearings where grit can get pushed inside.

★ Clean the chain with spray solvent and a rag while it is still on the bike.

★ Replace the chain every 3,000 to 4,000 miles. A worn chain is prone to skipping on a rear sprocket while you're pedaling out of the saddle.

★ Check for cracks in the frame, particularly stress points where tubes join at the head and bottom bracket. Signs of a crack include bulges in the metal and telltale cracks in the paint. If you find any frame cracks, have the problem evaluated by a professional mechanic.

★ Look for cracks in rims and cranksets. These should be replaced immediately.

★ Lubricate pivot points on front and rear derailleurs.

★ Lubricate pivot points on brakes and levers.

★ Check the headset for cracks.

Listen to
the COACH

Wrap your tools inside an old cotton tube sock before you put them in your saddle bag. This does several things. It protects your tube from tool punctures; it keeps everything else clean from tool grease; and it can be used as a makeshift glove to keep your action hand dirt-free during road repairs.

★ Check rack bolts and all add-ons for tightness.

★ Check the air pressure in air-sprung suspension forks.

★ Lift the fork boots and clean and lubricate the inner legs of suspension forks.

★ Check the condition of brake pads; replace if badly worn or excessively hard.

★ Clean brake pads and rims with alcohol.

★ Check tension on spokes; adjust as needed.

★ Check tightness of nuts on brake bodies, brake shoes, and cable anchors.

★ Lubricate the springs on clipless pedals with oil.

Cleaning a Bicycle

A clean bike looks nice, but that's only one of several benefits. You'll also find that it is easier to work on, smoother to ride, and lasts longer. Cleaning also helps you find faulty parts or frame defects before they become troublesome. This is one of the important reasons why Lance's mechanic washes his bike after each event. If you ride your bike 5 to 7 days a week, wash your bike every 2 weeks. If you ride less, wash your bike once a month.

You'll need a hose, two buckets, a small pan, sponges, rags, brushes of various sizes, detergent, fine steel wool or emery paper, and a solvent degreaser. Mark the brushes with colored tape so you can keep those used on greasy parts separate from the rest. A repair stand is helpful because you need to remove both wheels for thorough cleaning.

Here's how to clean your bike.

1. Put the bike on the stand and remove the wheels. If you plan to clean the chain without removing it, put the rear wheel's quick-release skewer or a long screwdriver through one of the triangular holes in the rear dropouts, through the chain, then through the opposite triangular hole. This holds the chain so you can turn the crankset without the chain scraping the right chainstay. Otherwise, remove the chain and put it in a pan of solvent.

2. Fill two buckets with water. Put a good household detergent in one and a mixture of detergent and solvent in the other. The detergent is for washing the bike. The mixture is for cleaning greasy parts.

3. Install a snap-on chain cleaner. If you don't have one but still want to clean the chain without removing it, spray it with solvent. Also apply solvent to the derailleurs, chainrings, and cogs. Don't use too much. Let it soak in. (Always squirt from above or below rather than from the side. Avoid spraying solvent or water directly at the hubs, headset, cassette body, pedals, and bottom bracket. Spraying them will contaminate bearing grease or wash it away, leading to wear.)

4. Turn the crankset to clean the chain. If you don't have a snap-on chain cleaner, use a stiff brush dipped in the detergent/solvent mixture to scrub the top and bottom of the chain as it passes over the screwdriver. It may take several revolutions of the chain to get it clean. Continue hand pedaling and scrubbing, periodically dipping the brush in the mixture.

5. Brush the derailleurs and chainrings with the mixture until they're clean.

6. Use the detergent bucket and a sponge to wash the rest of the bike. A small, narrow brush is handy for hard-to-reach spots.

7. Lay the rear wheel on the mixture bucket and brush the cogs. Be careful not to get any of the fluid on the rim or tire or into the bearings under the smallest and largest cogs. Slip a rag between each pair of cogs and slide it back and forth as if you're shining shoes, removing grime and excess solvent.

8. Wash both wheels. Hold them over the detergent bucket. Use sponges and brushes on the tires, rims, spokes, and hubs.

9. Rinse everything. Hold a hose or bucket of clean water above the bike and let a soft stream flow over the frame and parts. Do the same to the wheels.

10. Dry the bike with soft rags. Use separate rags for the drivetrain and frame and wheels.

11. Clean any rubber deposits from the sidewalls of both rims. Be sure to do this gently with fine steel wool or emery paper.

12. Apply polish to all painted and chrome parts or use wax, if desired. Follow the product's directions. Use Simichrome to polish aluminum parts if they're dull with oxidation.

13. Lubricate everything. Use a spray lube with a thin nozzle tube to spritz the brake and derailleur pivots and all points where cables enter or exit housings and touch guides or stops. Wipe off any excess. Also be sure to lubricate the chain if it remained on the bike during this cleaning.

14. Reassemble the bike. If you removed the chain to soak it, finish cleaning it with a brush. Wipe it down well, hang it to dry, apply lubrication, then wipe it again before you reinstall it.

Listen to the **COACH**

Sprinkle talcum powder on your spare clincher tube, put it in a resealable plastic sandwich bag, and place it in your bicycle tool bag. The spare tube with talcum powder will fit more easily in the tire when fixing a flat.

Fixing a Flat Tire

Most cyclists equip their wheels with clincher tires because they're light, reasonably priced, and easily maintained. Here's a simple routine to fix a flat and get you back on the road in 10 minutes.

1. Whenever a tire goes flat and needs repair, don't ride on it any farther. Push or carry your bike to a safe spot, then remove the wheel from the bike to repair the tire.

   Before taking the tire and tube apart, mark the tire next to the valve stem to establish the relationship between the tire and tube. This makes it easier later to locate any foreign matter still embedded in the tire casing.

2. If any air remains in the tire, let it out by pressing on the valve (unscrew the tip of a presta valve first). To minimize the chances of damaging the stem, start your tire removal on the side of the rim opposite the stem. Squeeze the sides of the tire toward the trough at the center of the rim to produce some slack, then hook a tire lever under the edge of the tire and pull it over the rim. But first, make sure your tire levers have no sharp edges that could further damage the tube. There are good plastic tire levers available that are less likely than many of the metal ones to damage a tube.

   Move a few inches along the rim and hook a second tire lever under the same side, also called bead, of the tire and pull it over the rim. If necessary, use a third tire lever. Once you get several inches of the tire diameter over the rim edge, you should be able to pull the rest of it over the rim by hand.

3. When one entire side of the tire is free from the rim, it's easy to remove the tube for repair. There is no need to take the tire completely off the rim at this point. Just push it over to one side while you remove the tube. Lift the tube's valve stem out of its rim hole, being careful not to damage it, then slip the remainder of the tube out of the tire and pull it away from the rim.

Pump some air into the tube and try to pinpoint the puncture by listening to or feeling with your fingers for the escaping air. Or, if a container of water is available, immerse the tube in the water and watch for air bubbles.

4. When you locate a repairable puncture, mark the tube at that point.

5. Pull the tire off the wheel and set it down. Line up the valve stem with the mark you previously made on the tire and spread the tube over the tire so the two are in the same relationship they had on the wheel. Check both the inside and outside of the tire casing at the point of the puncture. Remove any remnants of the offending object.

6. If you're unable to locate a puncture in your tube, check the valve stem. Tubes on underinflated tires can shift position, allowing the rim to cut into the side of the stem. If your stem is cracked or cut, you'll need to replace the tube.

7. Spread out the tube, and with the piece of sandpaper or the metal scraper from the tube repair kit, rough up the puncture area. Brush off any dust with your hand.

8. Coat the roughed area of the tube with a thin, even layer of glue that's a little larger in diameter than your patch. Make sure there are no globs, because they'll prevent the patch from sealing properly. After spreading the glue on your tube, allow it to dry completely. (This usually takes 5 minutes.)

Double Trouble

If you get a second flat while on the road, or strike a pothole with both front and rear wheels for double flats, it's time to use a patch kit.

- Remove the tube, pump air into it, and listen for a hiss, or feel with your fingers for escaping air. Some holes are difficult to pinpoint. Elusive culprits may be found by rubbing saliva over a suspicious place and watching for bubbles, or by holding an inflated tire close to your mouth to feel air escaping. If you happen to be near a stream or puddle, you can inflate the tube and run it under water to watch for escaping air bubbles. This works at home in the sink, too.

- Mark the spot where the tube is punctured.

- Rough up the puncture area with sandpaper from your tube repair kit. This helps the glue or glueless patch adhere more firmly to the tube. If you use glue, be sure to check on how long it needs to dry before applying the patch.

- Put on the patch. Press the patch down firmly to make sure it's on securely and covers the puncture.

9. Take a patch out of your repair kit. Choose a size that will cover the puncture and make good contact with the area all around it. Peel off the foil from the sticky side of the patch and fasten the patch in place on the tube.

10. To make sure you get a good seal, press down hard to force out any air bubbles. Inflate the tube enough to give it shape.

11. Push one side of the tire back onto the rim, leaving the other side and most of the casing hanging off the rim while you replace the tube. Temporarily push the second side of the tire over the rim at the valve hole and roll it back over the first side to uncover the hole. Fit the valve stem of the tube through the hole, then pull the

compressed section of the second tire side back over the tube and off the rim. Then, beginning at the stem area, work your way around the rim, tucking the tube back inside the tire.

12. Once the tube is in place, let the air out of it before you work the second side of the tire onto the rim. It's a good idea to start this process on the side of the rim opposite the stem and to end at the stem. This way, you'll be able to get the maximum possible slack in the tire when you need it for forcing the final few inches onto the rim. On very skinny tires, however, you may find it difficult to roll the final section of tire over the rim and seat it properly because of the thickness of the tube around the valve stem. If so, pull a section of tire back off the rim, take care of the stem area before the side gets excessively tight, and finish the job at a different location on the rim.

Try to avoid using tire levers to put the tire onto the rim. You should be able to do it with just your hands. If you use tire levers, you risk pinching the tube and damaging it. To get the slack you need for the final part of the process, go around the tire and squeeze the two sides together so they will drop down into the trough in the middle of the rim.

13. When you get to the last section of tire, you may find it quite difficult to force it onto the rim. Make sure you have given yourself all the available slack, then grasp the tire with both hands and, using a vigorous twisting motion of the wrists, try to roll the stubborn bit of side over the edge of the rim (see photo on page 34). If this technique does not work for you, push the side onto the rim bit by bit with your thumbs or the heels of your hands until it's completely on the rim.

Once the tire is on the rim, work around each side of the rim, rolling the tire back and looking to see if the

Use a vigorous twisting motion of the wrists to force the last stubborn section of tire over the rim.

tube is trapped beneath the side of the tire anywhere. If it is, the tube will get pinched and the tire won't seat properly when you inflate it (use a tire lever to poke the tube into the tire). If everything looks okay, pump 20 to 30 pounds of pressure into the tube. Check to make sure the stem is still straight and that the tire is seating properly. If it is, continue pumping until you bring the tire up to the recommended pressure (usually printed on the tire label).

4

Riding Position

In determining a rider's position, the most important aspect is comfort. As Lance has learned, no matter how aerodynamic his position is, if he isn't comfortable, he won't enjoy his ride or do his best. Lance's position on the bicycle has changed a lot since 1990, when he converted from triathlete to full-time cyclist. Your riding position will also evolve as your skills develop, your strength and confidence increase, and your flexibility improves. Riding positions depend on four factors.

★ Comfort

★ Biomechanics

★ Handling

★ Aerodynamics

Taken together, these factors constitute a dynamic balancing act. When Chris first joined the U.S. Cycling Federation staff, he looked ahead to the 1992 Barcelona Olympics and considered Lance as a candidate in the four-rider 100-kilometer (62.5 miles) team time trial. One look at Lance's riding position, however, convinced Chris that radical changes were needed. Lance leaned forward on his bicycle to take advantage of his strong thigh muscles. He used a triathlete's seatpost that slanted forward, in contrast to a road cyclist's seatpost that extends upright out of the frame's seat tube. Lance also had his handlebar stem down flush to the frame while his saddle was raised up high. The forward tilt compressed his body on the frame and arched his back, which increased his wind resistance.

With Chris's guidance, he started to change to a road rider's position. He exchanged his triathlete seatpost for a standard road cyclist's seatpost. Chris moved Lance's saddle farther back to distribute the young rider's workload and make greater use of his hamstrings, buttocks, calves, and lower-back muscles. Chris also raised Lance's stem a couple of inches out of the headset and lowered his saddle. These changes helped to flatten his back for more aerodynamic riding.

Eddy Merckx, the Belgian legend of the 1970s now synonymous with the bicycles bearing his name, worked with Lance in the early 1990s when Merckx supplied bicycles to the Motorola Cycling Team, Lance's first professional squad. Merckx has long been a stickler for proper positioning on a bicycle. The feature film *A Sunday in Hell*, about the 1976 Paris-Roubaix spring classic, shows Merckx pulling over to the side of the road during the race, getting off his bicycle, pulling out a wrench, loosening his seat bolt, and lowering his saddle only a fraction of an inch before getting back on his bicycle to resume racing. Merckx helped Lance refine his position to close to what it is today.

In 1996, Lance signed a contract to ride the next year with the French team Cofidis. He started working with that team's director, Cyrille Guimard, whose protégés included Tour de France champions Greg LeMond, Bernard Hinault, and Laurent Fignon. Guimard, a rival of Merckx's in their youth, modified Lance's riding position slightly. He also equipped Lance's bicycle with a handlebar narrower than the 42 centimeters to which he had been accustomed. The narrower handlebar gave him a more aerodynamic position by bringing his hands in closer. It also squeezed his chest to reduce his frontal exposure. Soon afterward, however, Lance was diagnosed with cancer, and the Cofidis team cancelled his contract.

When Lance recovered from his cancer treatment, he resumed training, with Chris's guidance. Lance began his comeback with the same position that Guimard had counseled. After a few hard rides, however, Lance began to complain of shooting pains in his chest.

Chris theorized that Lance's chest might be cramped and fitted Lance's bicycle with the 42-centimeter handlebar that he had used before. The wider handlebar moved his hands out and opened his chest. Shortly afterward, his chest pains disappeared. A more aerodynamic position isn't worth the sacrifice of comfort.

Comfort

Comfort varies greatly from person to person. It depends on factors such as individual flexibility and discrepancies such as feet that turn outward (supination), so that the outside of the foot bears the weight on the pedal, or inward (pronation), so that the inner edge of the foot bears the rider's body weight on the pedal.

Many cyclists are prone to lower-back stiffness after spending extended hours in the saddle, but Lance is even more susceptible. He has been diagnosed with a fracture of the fifth lumbar vertebrae, where the beltline crosses the small of the back. This condition, called spondylolisthesis, is considered congenital, but is common among weight lifters who do heavy shoulder squats and those who are active in their formative skeletal years.

To control his lower-back stiffness, Lance habitually performs stretching exercises and receives massages to keep the muscles relaxed. He pays particular attention to stretches for his lower back and hips. (For more information on stretching, see Recovery on page 92.)

Biomechanics

A rider's biomechanics, which refers to how each cyclist applies his power to pedaling, is another factor in determining a riding position. Everyone has a different biomechanical makeup. For example, Davis Phinney, Chris's teammate on the 7-Eleven Cycling Team that competed in the 1986 Tour de France, where Phinney became the first U.S. rider ever to win a stage there, rides with his toes pointed down. This is contrary to the conventional downstroke, where the foot moves parallel to the ground. Phinney pedals toe-down because he has larger quadriceps than normal. They act as powerful pistons that drive the pedals. Pedaling toe-down works for Phinney but may not work for others.

Lance's biomechanics rely on the strong quadriceps that he developed as a triathlete. As a result, he climbs faster while standing up than sitting down. Standing up, however, demands extra energy. Lance devoted considerable effort to improving his uphill riding from a seated position so that he could be competitive in the mountains of the 1999 Tour de France.

His biomechanics also explain why his back is rounded when he rides with his hands down on the drops of his handlebar and during time trials. He can't lean forward because of his lumbar fracture, and he compensates by hinging forward higher in his torso, resulting in a rounded upper back.

Handling

The third factor in riding position is handling, which refers to how a bicycle responds to maneuvers such as cornering, accelerating, and stopping. The feet, hands, and buttocks are the three points of contact that form the positioning triangle. How these points are positioned affects how you well you handle your bicycle.

You routinely shift position for balance and aerodynamics during a ride—depending on the landscape's rises and falls, wind conditions, curves in the road, and varying speeds. Once you're positioned properly on the bicycle, you're more comfortable and ready to change balance as the occasion demands.

Aerodynamics

The final factor is aerodynamics, which can reduce wind resistance and help raise speed. Some body positions are more aerodynamic than others. Lance rides time trials with his back rounded and his torso higher over the frame than most other professionals.

"Tests on Lance showed that the height of the rider on the bicycle is less important than the width of the rider," says Andrew Pruitt, Ed.D., director of the Boulder Center for Sports Medicine

Wind tunnel training.

in Colorado, who discovered Lance's fractured vertebrae in the early 1990s. "Staying narrow to cut through the air is better than riding low to the bike frame. Once someone is comfortable in the time trial position, even if he's not as aerodynamic as he would like, he'll go faster."

Steve Hed is a mechanic in suburban St. Paul, Minnesota, who has been a leader in designing aerodynamic deep-dish wheel rims that reduce resistance. During Lance's triathlon and amateur cycling career, he built Lance's bicycle wheels with the latest aerodynamic design and metals.

Hed cautions, however, that aerodynamic equipment has limits. "Riders in a group drafting behind one another have little need for aerodynamics because they don't do much work on their own. But when the pack breaks up and riders want to bridge across gaps, then it's important to make sure they have good aerodynamics. When they attack off the front in a race, aerodynamics are a key factor."

Position Basics

Obtaining the right position starts with a basic neutral position that serves as a benchmark. The neutral position distributes your weight evenly over the saddle, handlebar, and pedals. From there, you can modify your position to accommodate different terrain and conditions.

Once you've purchased a bicycle with a frame that fits properly (for more information, see Cycling Equipment on page 10), it's worth the time to make final adjustments for proper positioning.

"The bicycle needs to look like the rider who is going to ride it," says Dr. Pruitt, drawing on years of experience in treating patients who suffered knee and lower-back pains caused by improper riding positions. "A hero's bike doesn't fit everyone."

To reinforce his observation, Dr. Pruitt points out that Lance and his U.S. Postal Service teammates ride the same model bicycles and components. To the untrained eye, they may all look alike, but Lance's bicycle is set up for a different position than the bicycles ridden by George Hincapie, Kevin Livingston, Tyler Hamilton, and his other teammates.

Begin by fastening your bicycle onto a stationary trainer. Make sure that the front wheel hub is elevated to match the rear wheel hub in the stationary holder clamp. If you don't have access to a stationary trainer, have someone hold your bicycle upright.

Bike Positions

Saddle height. There are various formulas for this, but you needn't be a mathematician to know what the correct height looks like. Your knees should be slightly bent at the bottom of the pedal stroke, and your hips shouldn't rock on the saddle when viewed from behind. Here's a quick method that is used at the U.S. Olympic Training Center: Set the height so there is 5 millimeters of clearance between your heel and the pedal at the bottom of the stroke. Add a few millimeters if your shoes have very thin soles at the heel compared to the forefoot. Also, raise the saddle 2 millimeters to 3 millimeters if you have long feet in proportion to your height. For those who have knee pain caused by chondromalacia, a softening or wearing away and cracking of the cartilage under the kneecap that results in pain and inflammation, a saddle on the higher side of the acceptable range can be therapeutic, so gradually raise it until hip-rocking begins, then lower it slightly. Make saddle height changes 2 millimeters at a time to avoid leg strain.

Listen to the **COACH**

Try this after you've raised your saddle to make sure you haven't raised it too much. Put some loose change or a set of keys in a rear jersey pocket and listen for the sound of jingling, which would indicate a rocking upper body and shoulders. If that happens, lower the saddle slightly.

Fore/aft saddle position. The trend is to move the saddle back to produce more power for climbing. To start with, sit comfortably in the center of the saddle with the crankarms positioned horizontally. Drop a plumb line (a string with a small object attached) from the front of your forward kneecap. It should touch the center of the pedal axle. This is the neutral position, and you should be able to achieve it by loosening the seatpost clamp and sliding the saddle fore or aft. Climbers, time trialists, and some road racers prefer the line to fall a couple of centimeters behind the end of the crankarm to increase leverage in big gears. Conversely, track and criterium racers like a more forward position to improve leg speed. If your reach to the handlebar is wrong, use stem length to correct it, not fore/aft saddle position.

Saddle tilt. Eddy Merckx set Lance's saddle parallel with the top tube by using a carpenter's level, and Lance has used one since then for that purpose. For road riding and touring, a level saddle works best. A slight downward tilt may be more comfortable if you're using an extreme forward position with an aero bar and elbow rests, but too much tilt causes you to slide forward and place excessive weight on your arms.

Stem height. With the stem high enough (normally about an inch below the top of the saddle), you'll be more inclined to use the drops. Lowering it can improve aerodynamics, but may cramp your chest and make breathing difficult. Lance's stiff lower back makes it difficult for him to bend forward, so his stem is higher than those of many other pro riders. Never position the stem above its maximum extension line (usually etched in the side of the stem), or your

U.S. Postal Service Team member Frankie Andreu shows good position for descending. His hands are on the drops, elbows loose and knees bent to absorb road shock, and eyes forward on the road.

weight on the bar could cause it to break.

Top-tube and stem length. These combined dimensions, which determine your "reach," vary according to your flexibility and anatomy. There is no ultimate prescription, but there is a good starting point: When you're comfortably seated with elbows slightly bent and hands on the brake hoods, the front hub should be obscured by the handlebar. This is a relatively upright position, and with time, you may benefit from a longer stem extension to improve aerodynamics and flatten your back.

Another way to check stem length is to pedal easily on a stationary trainer and place your hands on the drops, as though you were racing or coasting downhill. When your knee is in the highest and most forward position, swing your elbow, slightly bent, toward the knee in the forward position. Your elbow and knee should just brush or have a small gap of up to an inch. If your elbow and knee overlap, the stem may be too short.

Stem size also depends on the length of the frame's top tube. Although road frames with the diamond shape may look alike, there are differences better measured with a ruler than the eye. For example, Italian frames tend to have top tubes either the same size as the seat tubes or 1 centimeter shorter. Some American manufacturers make top tubes up to 2 centimeters longer than seat tubes.

Women tend to have shorter torsos and arms than men, so Georgena Terry's bicycles have a top tube shorter than the seat tube.

Handlebar width. Bar width should equal shoulder width. Err on the side of a wider bar to open your chest for breathing. Some models are available with a large drop (vertical distance) to help big hands fit into the hooks. Position the bottom, flat portion of the bar horizontally or point it slightly down toward the rear brake.

Brake levers. Levers can be moved around the curve of the bar to give you the best compromise between holding the hoods and braking when your hands are in the bar hooks. Most riders do best if the lever tips touch a straightedge extended forward from under the flat, bottom portion of the bar.

Crankarm length. The trend is toward longer levers. These add power but may inhibit pedaling speed. In general, if your inseam is less than 29 inches, use 165-millimeter crankarms; 29 to 32 inches, 170-millimeter; 32 to 34 inches, 172.5-millimeter; and more than 34 inches, 175-millimeter. Crankarm length is measured from the center of the fixing bolt to the center of the pedal mounting hole. It's usually stamped on the back of the arm.

Listen to the COACH

Setting your stem height depends on your lower-back flexibility. Stand upright and then bend at the waist to touch your hands to the floor.

- If you can't touch the floor with your fingers, set the handlebar at the same height as the saddle.

- If you can touch the floor with the top halves of your fingers, set the handlebar 5 to 10 centimeters lower than the saddle.

- If you can set your palms flat on the floor, set the handlebar 10 to 15 centimeters below the saddle.

Bicycles for a Woman's Body

A man and a woman of the same height have different shoulder widths, torso lengths, and arm lengths, yet the majority of bicycles and their components are built for and tested by men. To address women's unique needs in cycling, two women have founded businesses to make cycling products and apparel that fit women.

In 1985, Georgena Terry founded Terry Precision Bicycles in Macedon, New York. "Our bicycles are sized to the bell curve of women's heights," says Terry, a mechanical engineer and a cyclist. "About 99 percent of women in the United States are from 4 feet 10 inches tall to 5 feet 10 inches tall. The average woman's height is 5 feet 4 inches. And she weighs 120 pounds to 130 pounds. So we take that as our starting point. Other bicycle manufacturers make frames for people who range from 5 feet 3 inches to 6 feet 2 inches. That leaves out a lot of women."

Terry Precision Bicycles start with smaller road and off-road frames to fit smaller women. The frames also feature top tubes significantly shorter than the seat tubes, a critical difference that helps most women more easily achieve a better riding position.

As popular as Terry Precision Bicycles have become, two-thirds of the company's business is derived from products made for women, such

Body Positions

Head and neck. Avoid putting your head down, especially when you're tired. Tilt your head side to side every once in a while to stretch and relax your neck muscles.

Upper body/shoulders. The less movement, the better. Imagine the calories burned by rocking side to side with every pedal stroke on a 25-mile ride. Use that energy for pedaling. Also, beware of creeping forward on the saddle and hunching your back when tired. Shift to a higher gear and stand to pedal periodically to prevent stiffness in your hips and back.

as saddles shaped to accommodate a wider pelvis, drop handlebars that feature a 1-centimeter indention on the inside of the curve to put the fingers closer to the brakes, and women's cycling apparel.

Another women's cycling product line was recently introduced by Wylder, Inc., in Santa Cruz, California. Their bicycles and components are called Juliana, for two-time world mountain bike champion and Olympic cyclist Juli Furtado, a co-owner of the company, who helped design the bicycles and components.

"Our saddles, handlebars, grips, and stems for both road and off-road bicycles are made for women's dimensions," explains Furtado. "After I retired from racing in 1997, I thought about what I wanted to do next. What I wanted was to make women-specific bikes and components. Women want different things from cycling than men. Women are out more for the aesthetic beauty of the ride, to enjoy the landscape and socialize with other riders. Women need to go into a bike shop and have a selection of women-specific products addressed to their size specifications."

Both Terry and Furtado agree that women place a higher premium on comfort rather than aerodynamics on the bicycle than men, and that greater comfort includes a more upright riding position.

Arms. Beware road rider's rigor mortis. Keep your elbows bent and relaxed to absorb shock and prevent veering when you hit a bump. Keep your arms in line with your body, not splayed to the side. This will help you to make a more compact, aerodynamic package.

Hands. Change hand position frequently to prevent finger numbness and upper-body stiffness. Grasp the handlebar firmly but gently; a white-knuckle hold on the bar is unnecessary and will produce energy-sapping muscle tension throughout the arms and shoulders.

★ Grasping the drops gives you maximum control *while* making it easier to apply the brakes and steer through turns. Also use them for descents and high-speed riding.

★ Holding the brake hoods, at the top of the bend of the handlebar, combines the best elements of both of the other positions to balance control with aerodynamics. Hands on the brake hoods are excellent for gaining better access to applying the brakes as well as for moderate climbing. Hands on the brake hoods also allow the rider to stand off the saddle when he hits a steep pitch.

★ On the tops, especially close to the stem, is one of Lance's favorite positions for climbing up hills because that helps him open up his chest and changes his hip angle to better use his hamstrings, calves, lower-back muscles, and arms.

★ When standing, grasp the hoods lightly and gently rock the bike side to side in sync with your pedal strokes. Always keep each thumb and a finger closed around the hood or bar to prevent losing your grip if you hit an unexpected bump.

Butt. By sliding backward or forward on the saddle, you can engage different muscle groups. This can be useful on a long climb. Moving forward emphasizes the quadriceps muscle on the front of the thigh, while moving back accentuates the opposite side, the hamstrings and glutes.

Feet. To prevent knee injury, strive for a cleat position that accommodates your natural foot angle, whether you're pigeon-toed or duck-footed. Make cleat adjustments on rides until you feel right, or pay a shop to do it using a fitting device. Better still, use a clipless pedal system that allows your feet to pivot freely ("float"), thus making precise adjustment unnecessary. Position the cleats fore/aft so that the widest part of each foot is directly above or slightly in front of the pedal axle.

5

Rules of the Road

Two weeks after winning the 1999 Tour de France, Lance accepted an invitation to visit Washington, D.C., to address the National Press Club as luncheon speaker and to meet President Clinton at the White House. National Press Club officers took their hard-shell cycling helmets to the luncheon. They sat at the head table with Lance and raised their helmets to show the audience their support for cycling. One reporter asked Lance how he coped with riding his bicycle in traffic dominated by cars, vans, motorcycles, and trucks. His reply: Motor vehicles more or less own the road, and cyclists borrow it.

Cyclists constantly hear from motorists who yell at them to get off the road, ride on the sidewalk, or otherwise find another place to ride. Nearly every time he goes out on his bicycle, Lance told the National Press Club, he hears these admonitions. He's also had some close calls that have led him to ride with even greater caution.

His worst such experience was with the driver of a pickup truck who ran him and a companion off the road while they were on a training ride near Austin, Texas. The driver was arrested for assault with a deadly weapon, convicted, and sentenced to jail. Lance told the National Press Club that he's learned to treat a problem motorist as a dangerous obstacle. He tries to avoid giving the motorist any excuse for hostile behavior.

Problems with motorists are not confined to the United

States. During a training ride in France in the spring of 1999, a driver accidentally struck Lance on his bicycle. The collision broke his bicycle frame and injured his shoulder. His training ride ended with a $100 cab bill to return to his home in Nice.

A common misperception among noncyclists is that different rules apply to cyclists and motorists. But according to state transportation laws, bicycles and cars are similar vehicles. Cyclists and motorists alike are subject to the same rules. Use of public roadways is a privilege, not a right.

When motorists and cyclists vie for access to the same roads, conflicts are inevitable. For safety reasons and to minimize conflicts, it's important that cyclists follow commonly acknowledged rules of the road.

The Rules

The first rule for safe cycling on public roads is to be sure drivers can see you. During the day, wear bright colors such as red, yellow, or orange. At night, wear white and use lights on the front and rear of your bicycle, plus reflectors. Once you're visible, use the following tips to make yourself even safer.

1. Ride defensively. This doesn't mean timidly. Be predictable and go about your business with a self-assurance that shows you know what you're doing. This helps motorists to anticipate your actions and feel comfortable sharing the road with you.

2. Ride well into the lane when traffic is stop-and-go. A cyclist can usually move as fast as cars in such conditions, so don't hug the curb where you're less visible and drivers are tempted to squeeze by.

3. Stay far enough in the traffic lane to avoid being struck by doors suddenly opening on cars that are parallel-parked. You'll likely hear some honks from following motorists who don't understand why you won't pull to the right to let them pass, but hold your ground. An opportunity to move right will come soon enough.

Listen to
the **COACH**

Developing proper traffic skills to navigate turns through multilane roads crowded with traffic takes practice. A good place to start navigating turns is on quiet secondary roads where traffic is light. Another technique is to visit high-density intersections at off-peak times, such as early weekend mornings, to gain familiarity with where to ride on the road to make turns. You can also follow an experienced friend or small group of experienced riders to see how they do it.

4. Don't gain ground at red lights by passing a line of cars on their right. It's illegal, and you can get "doored" from either side. It also irritates motorists because they have to pass you again after the light changes.

5. When you stop for a light, move to the center of your lane. This prevents drivers from edging forward, trapping you between them and the curb. When the light changes, accelerate to your cruising speed before moving right to allow them to pass.

6. Hold a straight line past cars that are intermittently parallel-parked. In other words, don't weave in and out of empty spaces. Drivers might not be ready for your sudden re-emergence in the traffic lane.

7. Beware of the three most common driver errors that threaten bike riders.

   ★ Turning left in front of an oncoming cyclist who's going straight through an intersection.

   ★ Failing to obey a stop sign and pulling out in front of a cyclist.

   ★ Passing a cyclist and immediately turning right, across the cyclist's path.

8. If you have the right of way at an intersection, don't coast through, or drivers may assume they can cut in front of you. Keep pedaling, but be prepared to brake.

9. For right turns, remain to the right side of the road but take care to prevent getting sandwiched between a vehicle coming up from the rear and the curb. For left turns, check with a quick look over your left shoulder to make sure that the path is clear. Then move laterally over to near the centerline of the road before continuing to the left to make your turn.

10. Use your hearing as an early-warning system. Tip-offs to danger include engines revving or slowing, squealing tires, and gear changes.

11. Help earn motorists' respect for cyclists by using hand signals for turns, lane changes, and stops. Forget that business about signaling right turns with the left arm held up. It originated because motorists can't reach across to point out the right window. Use your left arm (finger pointed) to signal left turns and braking (palm facing backward with arm at a downward angle). For right turns, hold out your right arm with finger pointed.

12. Look through the rear windows of parked cars for someone who might suddenly pull out into your lane or throw open a door. You also can spot a pedestrian who is about to step out from between cars.

13. Learn to scan each side street and driveway for cars, kids, and pets. Most potential hazards appear to the front when riding through a busy area.

14. When you see a car stopped at a cross street, watch its front wheels. That's the surest way to spot even slight forward movement. If you see any, get ready to brake, swerve, or yell.

15. Forget horns, bells, and whistles as warning devices in traffic. They take too long to use, and most aren't loud enough to be effective. A shout from deep in your diaphragm is instantaneous, requires no hands, and gets immediate attention.

16. Resist making an obscene gesture or shouting profanity on the rare occasion when a motorist intentionally harasses you. You may think you're doling out punishment, but psychologists say otherwise. It actually tells the hostile driver that he succeeded, and this encourages more of the same behavior. Likewise, don't meekly pull off the road. Retreating proves that you've been intimidated—another form of reward for the driver. The best response is no response. Keep riding as if nothing happened. No good can come from confrontations with hostile operators of big metal boxes.

17. If a threatening driver gives you the opportunity to read his license plate number, stop and report it to the local law enforcement agency as soon as you see a phone. Keep chanting the number so you won't forget it. Who knows—maybe the person has a bad driving record and this incident will be just what it takes to keep him off the road.

18. A useful skill in traffic is the "instant turn." This evasive action can prevent an accident when a car passes you and immediately turns right, across your path. It's also useful when an oncoming car turns left in front of you, leaving no time to brake. To initiate an instant turn, twitch your handlebar to the left to create a lean angle, then immediately dive into a right turn beside the car, avoiding a collision.

19. Beware of sun glare, a danger if you ride on busy roads early or late in the day. The low sun makes it difficult for motorists to see a cyclist. Eliminate this risk by altering your route so you don't ride directly into the sun.

Do the Bunnyhop

If you suddenly discover a small obstacle in your path, such as roadkill or a pothole, bunnyhop over it. Pull up on both sides of the handlebar while also pulling up on the pedals, which should be parallel to the ground (positioned at three o'clock and nine o'clock). Practice this move a couple of times to get comfortable with it before you use it.

20. When overtaking a slower cyclist, call out, "On your left," as a courtesy to reduce the chance of startling the slower rider. Continue moving ahead at least three bike lengths before moving laterally over to the right. Conversely, when overtaken, continue to ride a straight line and take care to protect your front wheel in case the passing cyclist cuts in front too soon.

21. Many local governments across America have converted old railroad beds to bike paths or have widened roads with designated bicycle lanes that take cyclists off the roads. Yet bike paths present their own hazards. Bike paths attract unskilled cyclists who may ride carelessly, inline skaters who speed faster than the conditions safely allow, and runners who may suddenly decide to stop or turn around. As always, ride cautiously on bike paths and observe the rules of the road. Any cyclist who wants to ride fast should consider a bike path only as a section of his commute to another road that will allow him to ride faster safely and without interruptions.

When the Worst Happens

Here's what you should do if you've been threatened or injured by a motorist.

★ Write down the license plate number of the offender. If you don't have a pad and pen, commit the license plate, or as much as possible, to memory.

★ Note as many details as possible about the vehicle's color, make, and model.

★ Note the driver's gender, race, and approximate age.

★ Note the location and time of day.

★ Look around for witnesses. Request business cards or ask whether they're listed in the telephone book and where they live to get in touch with them.

★ As soon as possible, write down these details while they're still fresh.

★ Promptly report as many details as noted to the police. They will track down the offending motorist. In case the motorist has fled the scene, the police record of the incident will identify a pattern that will help them to track down a chronic offender and potentially charge him with assault with a deadly weapon.

Accidents and How to Prevent Them

A study by the National Highway Traffic Safety Administration found that a majority of cycling accidents don't involve motor vehicles. Rather, most accidents involve cyclists falling down by themselves as a result of poor handling skills, equipment failures, or ignorance of how to ride in traffic. Most of these accidents are preventable. Here's how to prevent the most common types of accidents.

Cause: You hit an obstruction such as a parked car or pothole. *Prevention:*

★ Look ahead to gain time for maneuvering around potholes, parked cars, or other hazards. Spot them in advance to steer clear.

★ If there's no time to navigate around small obstacles, bunnyhop over them.

★ Keep a firm grip on the handlebar to stay in control when the front wheel abruptly hits something.

Cause: A motorist suddenly pulls in front of you or opens a door in your path.
Prevention:

★ Allow a margin of a few feet when passing parked vehicles.

★ Make an emergency stop. The front brake gives the best stopping power, but you must be careful not to catapult over the handlebar. An alternative is to rise out of the saddle and put your butt over the rear wheel for balance, apply the rear brake, and pull the bicycle back between your legs.

★ Practice emergency stops to gain confidence.

Cause: You pull onto a road without yielding to oncoming traffic.
Prevention:

★ Look in both directions before turning into traffic and wait till the road is clear. Motorists tend to look up the road for moving traffic rather than looking to the curb for cyclists.

★ Don't assume that motorists see you. Drivers may be distracted while behind the wheel, listening to music, or talking on a cell phone.

★ Always ride defensively.

Cause: A motorist turns abruptly.
Prevention:

★ When a motorist passes, allow the vehicle to move ahead so that if it suddenly crowds in or starts to turn, you have time and distance to either apply the brakes and fall behind or to turn with the vehicle.

★ Execute an emergency stop.

Cause: The roads are wet from rain.
Prevention:

★ Ride with caution in the first hour after it starts raining; roads are very slick as a result of water mixing with oil film from vehicular exhaust.

★ Allow extra time and distance to apply your brakes.

★ Exercise greater care on turns.

★ Stay alert to standing water that might conceal a hole. When at all possible, ride around puddles.

★ Don't execute turns over road paint and metal road hazards such as sewer drains and manhole covers. These items become very slick when it rains.

The
Carmichael
Training
System

PART
TWO

6

The Heart of Training

Both Chris and Lance firmly believe that the portable heart rate monitor (HRM) and powermeters are the most helpful tool that a cyclist can buy to improve the efficiency of his training. They allow a rider to assess his fitness level and determine the correct training intensities that even 15 years ago, would have been available only to elite cyclists.

Lance is never far from his HRM—he wears it on 90 percent of his rides to continually monitor both his efforts and his recovery. For Lance, wearing an HRM is like having his coach along for every ride.

Here's a sampling of the many ways these tools will improve your training.

Maximize your maximum. Determining your maximum sustainable heart rate (MSHR) or maximum sustainable power (MSP) is the first step toward defining correct intensities. It's also the basis for The 7-Week Success Plan on page 70. A heart rate monitor allows you to pinpoint your MHR with much more accuracy than the outdated (but still widely used) "220 minus your age" formula, which is useful only as a general guideline.

Get more power from less work. Without a powermeter or HRM, it's difficult to track the actual intensity of your training

What Would
LANCE Do?

I use heart rate ceilings for my training rides. They keep me in my upper aerobic capacity to avoid crossing my lactate threshold, which is when the body can no longer process oxygen quickly enough to remove waste products associated with energy production. The object is to end my training ride having ridden almost entirely aerobically, so I ride within a narrow range of 5 beats, based on a certain percentage of my maximum heart rate. For example, I do my interval workouts by staying in the range of 160 to 164 beats per minute.

because both heart rate and power fluctuate wildly on a ride—low when cruising downhill, through the roof when climbing a steep hill. By recording your average heart rate and power output, these tools allow you to track your fitness level clearly over time. For example, if your average heart rate gets lower over the course of several weeks—given the same pace and riding conditions—it's a clear sign your performance level is improving. Similarly, when your average power output increases, it's a clear sign you're getting stronger and faster.

Tame those pesky intervals. Either a powermeter or HRM can help manage your interval sessions by indicating when to work and when to recover, with all of the essential data automatically recorded for later entry in your training log. You're left only to concentrate on the arduous task at hand, rather than having to expend brainpower tracking how many intervals you've done for how long.

Ride the road to recovery. Rest and recovery are two sides of the same wheel. The harder and more exhausting your training is, the longer it will take you to recover. Conversely, the fitter you are, the faster you'll bounce back. To force himself to take it easy on his designated recovery days, Lance sets the monitor's alarm to stay under a certain limit—in his case, 120 beats per minute—allowing his muscles to rest up for the next week's workouts.

Stay in the range. Set the alarm for your upper and lower target heart rates, and you'll know immediately—without looking down—whether you're riding in the proper range for that workout. You're doing fine as long as the alarm doesn't sound.

Know your limits. Some HRMs allow you to set more than one heart rate limit. Lance, for example, finds it helpful to set different limits for the three phases of a workout—warmup, main exercise period, and cooldown. (Alternatively, such settings might be useful for a triathlon event, with different limits used in the swimming, cycling, and running portions.)

Override your programming. The training schedule says that your hard-earned week of recovery is over and it's time to get back to work on some tempo training. But after taking your waking heart rate, you find that it's still three to six beats above your normal baseline, and has been all week. Should you listen to the calendar or your heart? Definitely listen to your heart, because an elevated waking pulse is a sure sign that your body is still recovering. Dedicate that day to another recovery ride.

Outsmart your brain. You've been riding hard and feeling good. So good, in fact, that your recovery days seem slow and tedious—so you've been skipping them altogether. But lately, even though you don't feel particularly tired, you've been having trouble raising your heart rate to the correct levels for your workouts. If you're using a powermeter, you'll notice that the effort

Listen to the COACH

There's a short gap between the start of exertion and the response from your heart. For example, if you're riding along at 140 beats per minute and you suddenly begin to sprint, your effort jumps way up immediately—but your heart rate response lags behind.

Listen to the COACH

Your maximum and maximum sustainable heart rate have no relationship to your actual cycling performance. They also vary widely among individuals of similar fitness levels. Lance's teammate George Hincapie, 2 years younger than Lance, can easily cruise along at a hummingbird-like heart rate of 185 bpm. At that rate, however, Lance is near his maximum threshold.

necessary to reach your workout power ranges is much higher than normal. These are sure signs of overtraining—and clear indicators that you're long overdue for a week of recovery.

Step up the action. When you finish a day's worth of training, you feel tired—so you must be working hard. But even after weeks of riding, your heart rate still skyrockets as soon as you hit that killer hill on the way home. What gives? Time to add more hills to your training load—and increase workout intensity all around. Be fastidious about staying within the proper training ranges. What you perceive to be a beneficial workout may actually be wasted effort.

The Workings of a Heart Rate Monitor

A heart rate monitor is a lightweight computer with two parts. The wireless transmitter is attached to a band that wraps around the chest. The transmitter rests over your sternum, just under the pectoral muscles. The band should be snug enough not to move while you ride, but should never restrict your breathing. Simply put, you shouldn't notice it once you put it on.

Like a stethoscope, the transmitter "listens" to the heartbeat and sends it continuously and wirelessly to the receiver, a watchlike device worn either on the wrist or mounted to the handlebar, depending on your preference. The transmitter can't be moved more than 3 feet from the receiver without losing the signal.

Heart rate monitors gather data from your body in one of two ways. The most effective transmitters use electrodes that read the natural fluctuations of electrical signals in your skin—voltage changes that occur as your heart beats. Perspiration actually enhances the connection between the skin on your chest and the electrodes on the transmitter.

In contrast, pulse meters (photo-reflectance models) use sensors to measure the mechanical pulse of the bloodflow through your capillaries. This information is then converted into a beat-per-minute readout.

What to Look For in a Heart Rate Monitor

Heart rate monitors are designed with a pulse-pounding range of data functions. The more functions, the more expensive the monitor. Here's a list of features you can expect to find.

Must-Have Features

Target heart rate zone alarms
Elapsed time in target zone
Average/maximum/minimum heart rate per trip
Total training time
Stopwatch

Nice-to-Have Features

Upload/download data to computer
Heart rate over multiple intervals/laps
Time spent in programmed HR ranges
Recovery heart rate/time
Calories burned counter
Countdown timer
Backlit LCD display
Heart rate sampling over a specified time period

Cyclecomputer Features

If you'll be relying on the services of both a cyclecomputer and a heart rate monitor, save handlebar real estate by buying an HRM

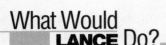

What Would LANCE Do?

I consider my heart rates for different activities to be very important indicators of how my training is progressing. Here are some of those heart rates.

Maximum heart rate: 201

Lactate threshold heart rate: 178

Time trial heart rate: 188 to 192

Average heart rate during endurance rides (4 to 6 hours): 124 to 128

model that incorporates the standard functions of both, including:

Clock
Trip time
Trip distance
Odometer
Average speed
Maximum speed
Cadence
Dual bike setup (allows you to switch easily between two
    different bikes without reconfiguring the settings)

The Workings of a Powermeter

Powermeters have been used by the pros for several years, and now they are widely accessible to the general public. These devices are mounted on the bicycle and allow you to closely monitor your actual workload during rides. Typically there are three parts to these pieces of equipment: a heart rate transmitter, a handlebar mounted computer, and the actual powermeter.

The transmitter is the same type as the one used with a standard heart rate monitor and the handlebar computer displays current/average speed, current/average cadence, current/average/

maximum heart rate, current/average/maximum power, trip/total distance, and more. You can download all of this information to your computer so you can track your progress. The most important piece is the actual powermeter, as this is where the workload is measured on the bike.

Inside the powermeter, strain gauges provide the measuring component. Strain gauges are essentially thin pieces of metal that bend or deform in response to the forces or torques applied to them, which in this case are the forces applied by your legs. The two most popular powermeters have the strain gauges located in cranks (SRM) and the rear hub (Power Tap). The handlebar computer then uses the torque data in conjunction pedal cadence (angular velocity) to display a power output in Watts.

Torque × Angular Velocity = Power in Watts

In order to produce more power, you can push harder on the pedals, pedal faster, or a combination of those two. The goal of training is to increase your MSP, or the amount of work you can do on the bike for a prolonged period of time. For instance, if you can ride at 200 Watts for 10 minutes now, you'll go faster when your training enables you to ride at 220 watts for 10 minutes.

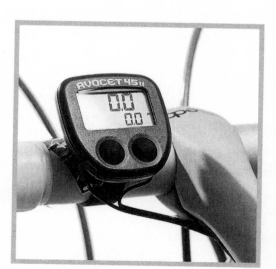

A powermeter measures both workload and time, which can also be expressed as the amount of energy, in kilojoules, that you're producing. We know that one calorie equals about four kilojoules

A handlebar cyclecomputer is essential for keeping accurate training data.

Essential Training Log Data

Ride Information

Specific ride goals

Date

Route

Time out/in

Elapsed time

Ride mileage

Cumulative mileage

Body Information

Waking heart rate (before getting out of bed)

Morning body weight (after bathroom)

Average heart rate (after ride)

Actual workouts performed (hills, tempo, intervals, sprints, recovery)

Other Data

This information is not essential, but by including such data, you'll develop a more well-rounded view of your training progress.

Average speed

Maximum speed

Cumulative on-bike time

Weather conditions (temperature, wind speed, precipitation)

Mental disposition, on a scale of 1 to 5 (5=On top of the world; 1=Should have stayed home)

Perceived exertion, on a scale of 1 to 5 (5=Nothing left in the tank; 1=Didn't break a sweat)

Noteworthy news (Chased by a Doberman, finally won town-line sprint, blew two tires, found $20) and that the human body is about 25% efficient on the bicycle. This means that 25% of the energy is used to propel the bike and the other 75% is given off as heat. In turn, this means that the kilojoules you produce on the bike are roughly equal to the number of calories you burned during your ride. You can use this information to balance your caloric intake with your exercise volume and intensity. You can also gauge the true intensity of your ride. A one-hour ride at 18 mph can produce a high kilojoule total if you're riding into a headwind, but the same hour at the same speed on the same route can be easier and produce a lower kilojoule total on a windless day.

The biggest benefit to using a powermeter is that you can record the true demands of your events and then use that information to design training that prepares you for them. You can examine an event power file to see the power outputs that were required at key times, like a big climb, and then you can use this information to target your training. For example, if you review an event file and determine that you spent 15 minutes at VO_2 intensity, then in order to overload that system you will need to accomplish more than 15 minutes of work at VO_2 intensity in your training. This could be done in the form of 6×3 minutes at PowerInterval intensity or a total of 18 minutes of work time.

The powermeter can also be very useful in regard to recovery. Workouts are only effective when you can maintain the right power output, so once you are unable to maintain those powers, it's time to end the workout and focus on recovery. If you planned on doing five intervals and your power falls significantly during the third, there's no benefit to doing numbers four and five. Go home and rest, your powermeter is letting you know that you sufficiently overloaded your body and you now need recovery time so your body can adapt to the training.

Recording and Tracking Your Progress

Lance is diligent about his training log. He and Chris record his heart rate, distance, cadence, and other key data as daily snapshots of his naturally fluctuating training levels. Analyzed over the course of weeks and months, this diary gives him an unsurpassed view of his progress—analysis that would be impossible if he tried to keep every slippery number in his head.

Compare, for example, the insight you gain from the subjective description, "I did intervals today and trained pretty hard" with this objective record: "Today, I spent 2 hours at 70 percent maximum sustainable heart rate. I did three 3-minute intervals at 92 percent MSHR, each separated by 3 minutes of recovery." Only a training log can consistently provide this kind of no-nonsense information.

Chris credits Lance's phenomenal success in the time trials of the 1999 Tour de France in large part to analysis of his training log. In early-season time trial training, Lance preferred to push big gears at a relatively slow cadence of 75 to 85 rpm—conventional wisdom for time trial technique.

By tracking Lance's daily numbers, however, Chris soon realized that Lance produced more power by pedaling smaller gears at a faster cadence, around 105 rpm. This breakthrough led to surprising victories in both of the Tour's time trials (and the opening prologue—a hat trick matched only by five-time Tour winners Eddy Merckx, Bernard Hinault, and Miguel Indurain).

You can buy an off-the-shelf cycling training diary like The

Chris performs a wireless download of training data from Lance's heart rate monitor to a laptop computer.

Carmichael Training Systems Cyclist's Diary (see page 247), or create your own with a spiral notebook or computer, using the headings given in "Essential Training Log Data." Or go cyber with a training log Web site or cycling-specific software. (Look for software programs that accept direct downloads from your heart rate monitor or cyclecomputer. This feature eliminates the need to enter the information by hand.)

7

The 7-Week Success Plan

Are you looking to beat the best rider in your club at the district championships—or do you just want to whup him once and for all in the town-line sprint? Want to complete your first 5-hour century—or just shed a few pounds and increase your average speed? The Carmichael Training System 7-Week Success Plan is designed to help you unlock your cycling potential with three specialized weekly training programs that build on your current fitness level, no matter what it is.

Chris developed this method of training from the experience he gained over 10 years of coaching Lance and hundreds of elite men and women athletes for the Olympic Games, World Championships, and the Tour de France. His philosophy is to train with a particular target in mind—what he calls bull's-eye training—over a 7-week period of steadily increasing intensity.

He noticed early on that athletes hold their mental and physical focus best if they aim for a specific goal at the end of a relatively short window. In 1998, for example, after missing almost 3 months of serious competition, Lance set his sights on the last event of the season: the World Championships. Seven weeks later, he was supercharged with a new sense of motivation, desire, and commitment to succeed. When the time came to put up or shut up, Lance rode to an impressive fourth-place finish in both the time trial and the road race.

By following these proven programs, you too can get fit, stay focused, feed your hunger to succeed, and arrive at the start line ready to fly. Chris designed these programs to be successive—you can progress from one to the next. Just be sure to include a week of recovery riding between each program.

Field Test for Fitness

Before starting the 7-week program, you must determine your level of fitness. The Carmichael Training Systems Field Test for Fitness provides you with a quick and simple way to determine the appropriate training program and intensity ranges for you. This test is for riders of all age groups and levels of fitness. And, best of all, it requires nothing more than a bicycle and a stretch of flat road.

The test is essentially a 3-mile time trial. In other words, you'll need to ride as hard as you possibly can for 15,840 feet. You then match your result with the times on page 72 to find your ideal training category. You'll also use the average heart rate and power output to determine your training intensities. Later in the season, you'll take the test again to re-evaluate your place in the program.

Step one: Find a test course. Locate and measure a 3-mile course that's as flat as possible and isn't busy with traffic. Try to choose a day when the wind is relatively calm and the temperature is warm but not hot. Conditions are usually more favorable in the early evening.

Step two: Fuel properly. Do not eat for at least 2 hours before taking the test. Forty minutes prior to the test, drink a high-carbohydrate sports drink to stay hydrated.

Step three: Warm up. For 10 to 20 minutes, ride hard enough to sweat, but not as hard as you can.

Step four: Start the ride right. Ask a friend to hold you in position at the start. Place the crankarm of your strongest leg at the two o'clock position to get the most power out of your first pedal stroke. If no one is holding you, roll up to the start line slowly. Select a gear that allows a quick, stable start. Pedal standing out of the saddle to build speed more quickly. When you hit top pedal cadence in your starting gear, sit down and prepare to gear up. Don't start too fast. Allow at least 2 minutes to reach top speed.

Step five: Find the ideal gear. Select a gear that allows you to maintain a cadence of 80 to 90 rpm. Avoid the impulse to mash a big gear at slow rpm. The greater resistance will allow more leg-burning lactic acid to develop. The secret is to use the gearing that is most efficient for your personal riding style. This will take some experimenting. Watch your speed and heart rate in different gears to establish optimum pedal cadence.

Step six: Feel the burn. Settle into a steady rhythm of breathing. From here on, it's going to hurt. If it isn't hard and painful at this point, you need to pedal harder and faster.

Step seven: Get an exact time. Time your 3-mile ride to the nearest second. Record the weather conditions, gearing used, and perceived effort (rated from 1 to 10, with 1 being the easiest) for the test. If you're using a powermeter, record the average power for the test.

Step eight: Cool down. Finish the test with an easy ride of 15 to 30 minutes of easy pedaling to flush the body of lactic acid.

Step nine: Determine your training ranges. Take the average heart rate (MSHR) and power, if applicable, for your field test effort. Determine your training ranges using the following table.

Men—Recreational Cyclist

Fitness Test Time	Fitness Category
Less than 10 minutes	Beginner to Intermediate
More than 10 minutes	Beginner

Men—Racing Cyclist

Fitness Test Time	Fitness Category
Less than 8 minutes	Intermediate to Advanced
More than 8 minutes	Intermediate

Women—Recreational Cyclist

Fitness Test Time	Fitness Category
Less than 12 minutes	Beginner to Intermediate
More than 12 minutes	Beginner

Women—Racing Cyclist

Fitness Test Time	Fitness Category
Less than 10 minutes	Intermediate to Advanced
More than 10 minutes	Intermediate

Do It Again

Retest yourself later in the season to assess your fitness improvement to fine-tune your training ranges. When you do retest, ride the same 3-mile course under similar conditions and with the same bicycle.

Workouts

Chris developed an entire arsenal of workouts that made Lance the champion he is today. For the three Carmichael Training System programs in this chapter, Chris focused on four workouts—Tempo, FastPedal, PowerIntervals, and FlatSprints—which will transform you into a strong, efficient rider.

Tempo™

Goal: Raise your aerobic capacity

How: Cadence should be relatively low—try a range of 70 to 85 rpm while remaining within the correct training intensity. This increases pedal resistance and helps strengthen your leg muscles. Stay in the saddle when you hit hills during your tempo workouts to bolster the connective tissues and supporting muscle groups. Soon, your training will develop into more explosive workouts that can put undue strain on unprepared joints. It's important to ride

Training Zones

Ranges	% MSHR	% FT Average Power	Description
1	50–70	30–50	Easy riding, recovery training
2	50–91	45–73	Endurance base training
3	88–90	81–85	Aerobic capacity training
4	92–94	85–90	Lactate threshold training
5	94+	90+	Maximum aerobic training, increasing max VO_2

the entire length of the tempo workout with as few interruptions as possible to strengthen and bolster your joints.

Training intensity: Range 3 (HR: 88–90% MSHR, Power: 81–85% MSP)

FastPedal™

Goal: Improve your pedaling efficiency

How: Find a relatively flat road. Gearing should be light and pedal resistance low. Slowly increase your cadence, starting out with 15 to 18 revolutions over 10 seconds (90 to 108 rpm). Increase cadence while staying in the saddle. Keep your hips smooth; don't rock them from side to side. Concentrate on pulling through the bottom of the pedal stroke and over the top.

Training intensity: Fastest cadence should be 18 to 20 revolutions in 10 seconds (108 to 120 rpm)

PowerIntervals™

Goal: Increase your max VO_2

How: On an indoor trainer or a long, uninterrupted stretch of flat road, pick a gear that allows a cadence of 110 or higher. Take 1 minute to build to the desired training zone and maintain that intensity for the remaining interval. The last 2 minutes of each interval will develop your max VO_2. If you must, shift into an easier gear to maintain the cadence, but don't drop the intensity—a high heart rate will train your body to deliver more oxygen to your muscles. Recover in between by spinning freely in easy gears.

Listen to the COACH

Your performance levels may decline in weeks 2 and 3 as the training load taxes your system, working its magic on your body. Week 4 is dedicated to recovery and regeneration to prepare you for the rigors of the last 3 weeks of hard effort.

Training intensity: Three-minute intervals in Range 5 (above 94% MSHR or above 90% MSP), with a 3-minute recovery between efforts

FlatSprints™

Goal: Boost your jump speed

How: Sprints are always performed at 100 percent maximum output. On flat terrain, roll along at a moderate speed (15 to 22 mph, depending on your level of development) in an easy gear. Jump out of the saddle, accelerating the entire time. Return to the saddle after a few seconds—maintaining high pedal speed— and focus on a smooth and efficient form for the rest of the sprint.

Training intensity: Sprints should last 10 to 12 all-out seconds, with 5 to 10 minutes for recovery between each sprint

Program Levels

Beginner

This program is designed to improve your general aerobic conditioning—the ideal starting place for cyclists who haven't trained at all in the last year or more. Workout intensity is easy to moderate and takes you to progressively higher levels of aerobic fitness.

Goal: Improved aerobic conditioning

Weekly training: 6 to 8 hours

Intensity: 50 to 90 percent of MSHR, 50 to 80 percent of MSP

Intermediate

Start here if you ride a lot but lack a training focus. This program increases your lactate threshold so that you can ride at faster speeds without building up lactic acid from pedaling anaerobically.

Goal: Faster sustained riding pace

Weekly training: 8 to 10 hours

Intensity: 50 to 94 percent of MSHR, 50 to 90 percent of MSP

Advanced

This program is designed for the fit cyclist who wants to tackle a specific goal—a late-season race, for example. You'll increase your overall speed so you can handle the constant changes in pace while attacking and counterattacking.

Beginner

	Monday	Tuesday	Wednesday
Week one	30 minutes in Zone 1 on flat terrain at steady, easy pace.	45 minutes in Zone 2 with 5 minutes Fast-Pedal on flat terrain.	1 hour in Zone 2 on flat terrain; pedal at 80–85 rpm the entire ride.
Week two	30 minutes in Zone 2 with 10 minutes Fast-Pedal on flat terrain.	45 minutes in Zone 2 with 5 minutes Fast-Pedal on flat terrain.	1 hour in Zone 2 on flat terrain; pedal at 80–85 rpm the entire ride.
Week three	30 minutes in Zone 2 with 10 minutes Fast-Pedal on flat terrain.	45 minutes in Zone 2 with 10 minutes Fast-Pedal on flat terrain.	1 hour in Zone 2 on flat terrain; pedal at 80–85 rpm the entire ride.
Week four	30 minutes in Zone 1; recovery ride.	30 minutes in Zone 1; recovery ride.	Day off
Week five	30 minutes in Zone 2 with 10 minutes Fast-Pedal on flat terrain.	45 minutes in Zone 2 with 10 minutes of Tempo.	1 hour in Zone 2 on flat terrain; pedal at 80–85 rpm the entire ride.
Week six	30 minutes in Zone 2 with 10 minutes Fast-Pedal on flat terrain.	45 minutes in Zone 2 with 15 minutes of Tempo.	1 hour in Zone 2 on flat terrain; pedal at 80–85 rpm the entire ride.
Week seven	30 minutes in Zone 2 with 10 minutes Fast-Pedal on flat terrain.	45 minutes in Zone 2 with 15 minutes of Tempo.	1 hour in Zone 2 on flat terrain; pedal at 80–85 rpm the entire ride.

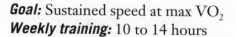

Goal: Sustained speed at max VO_2
Weekly training: 10 to 14 hours
Intensity: 50 to 94+ percent of MSHR, 50 to 90+ percent of MSP

Thursday	Friday	Saturday	Sunday
45 minutes in Zone 2 with 5 minutes Fast-Pedal on flat terrain.	Day off	1 hour in Zone 2 with 10 minutes Fast-Pedal on flat terrain.	1½ hours in Zone 2 on hilly terrain; try to stay in the saddle while climbing hills.
45 minutes in Zone 2 with 5 minutes Fast-Pedal on flat terrain.	Day off	1 hour in Zone 2 with 10 minutes Fast-Pedal on flat terrain.	1½ hours in Zone 2 on hilly terrain; try to stay in the saddle while climbing hills.
45 minutes in Zone 2 with 5 minutes Fast-Pedal on flat terrain.	Day off	1 hour in Zone 2 with 10 minutes Fast-Pedal on flat terrain.	2 hours in Zone 2 on hilly terrain; push into Zone 3 on the hills.
30 minutes in Zone 1; recovery ride.	45 minutes in Zone 2 with 2 FlatSprints of 10 seconds each with 10 minutes recovery between sprints.	1 hour in Zone 2 with 10 minutes Fast-Pedal on flat terrain.	1 hour in Zone 2 on hilly terrain; push into Zone 3 on the hills.
45 minutes in Zone 2 with 5 minutes Fast-Pedal on flat terrain.	Day off	1 hour in Zone 2 with 10 minutes Fast-Pedal on flat terrain.	1½ hours in Zone 2 with 15 minutes of Tempo.
45 minutes in Zone 2 with 5 minutes Fast-Pedal on flat terrain.	Day off	1 hour in Zone 2 with 10 minutes Fast-Pedal on flat terrain.	1½ hours in Zone 2 with 20 minutes of Tempo.
45 minutes in Zone 2 with 5 minutes Fast-Pedal on flat terrain.	Day off	1 hour in Zone 2 with 10 minutes Fast-Pedal on flat terrain.	1½ hours in Zone 2 with 30 minutes of Tempo.

Intermediate

	Monday	Tuesday	Wednesday
Week one	Day off	1 hour in Zone 2 with 10 minutes Tempo on flat terrain.	30 minutes in Zone 1; recovery ride.
Week two	Day off	1 hour in Zone 2 with 15 minutes Tempo on flat terrain.	30 minutes in Zone 1; recovery ride.
Week three	Day off	1 hour in Zone 2 with 20 minutes Tempo on flat terrain.	30 minutes in Zone 1; recovery ride.
Week four	Day off	30 minutes in Zone 1; recovery ride.	30 minutes in Zone 1; recovery ride.
Week five	Day off	1 hour in Zone 2 with 30 minutes Tempo on flat terrain.	30 minutes in Zone 1; recovery ride.
Week six	Day off	1 hour in Zone 2 with 30 minutes Tempo on flat terrain.	30 minutes in Zone 1; recovery ride.
Week seven	Day off	1 hour in Zone 2 with 30 minutes Tempo on flat terrain.	30 minutes in Zone 1; recovery ride.

Thursday	Friday	Saturday	Sunday
1 hour in Zone 2 with 10 minutes Tempo on flat terrain.	45 minutes in Zone 2 with 10 minutes Fast-Pedal on flat terrain.	1 hour in Zone 2 with 15 minutes Tempo on flat terrain.	1½ hours in Zone 2 with 20 minutes Tempo on hilly terrain.
1 hour in Zone 2 with 10 minutes Tempo on flat terrain.	45 minutes in Zone 2 with 10 minutes Fast-Pedal on flat terrain.	1 hour in Zone 2 with 15 minutes Tempo on flat terrain.	1½ hours in Zone 2 with 25 minutes Tempo on hilly terrain.
1 hour in Zone 2 with 15 minutes Tempo on flat terrain.	45 minutes in Zone 2 with 10 minutes Fast-Pedal on flat terrain.	1 hour in Zone 2 with 15 minutes Tempo on flat terrain.	1½ hours in Zone 2 with 30 minutes Tempo on hilly terrain.
30 minutes in Zone 1; recovery ride.	1 hour in Zone 2 with 3 FlatSprints of 10 seconds each with 10 minutes recovery between sprints.	1 hour in Zone 2 with 15 minutes Tempo on flat terrain.	1½ hours in Zone 2 with 30 minutes Tempo on hilly terrain.
1 hour in Zone 2 with 20 minutes Tempo on flat terrain.	45 minutes in Zone 2 with 10 minutes Fast-Pedal on flat terrain.	1 hour in Zone 2 with 20 minutes Tempo on flat terrain.	1½ hours in Zone 2 with 40 minutes Tempo on hilly terrain.
1 hour in Zone 2 with 20 minutes Tempo on flat terrain.	45 minutes in Zone 2 with 10 minutes Fast-Pedal on flat terrain.	1 hour in Zone 2 with 20 minutes Tempo on flat terrain.	1½ hours in Zone 2 with 50 minutes Tempo on hilly terrain.
1 hour in Zone 2 with 20 minutes Tempo on flat terrain.	45 minutes in Zone 2 with 10 minutes Fast-Pedal on flat terrain.	1 hour in Zone 2 with 20 minutes Tempo on flat terrain.	1½ hours in Zone 2 with 60 minutes Tempo on hilly terrain.

Advanced

	Monday	Tuesday	Wednesday
Week one	30–45 minutes in Zone 1 with steady easy spinning on flat terrain.	30–45 minutes in Zone 1 with steady easy spinning on flat terrain.	30–45 minutes in Zone 1 with steady easy spinning on flat terrain.
Week two	30–45 minutes in Zone 1 with steady easy spinning on flat terrain.	30–45 minutes in Zone 1 with steady easy spinning on flat terrain.	30–45 minutes in Zone 1 with steady easy spinning on flat terrain.
Week three	30–45 minutes in Zone 1 with steady easy spinning on flat terrain.	30–45 minutes in Zone 1 with steady easy spinning on flat terrain.	30–45 minutes in Zone 1 with steady easy spinning on flat terrain.
Week four	30–45 minutes in Zone 1; recovery ride.	30–45 minutes in Zone 1; recovery ride.	Day off
Week five	30–45 minutes in Zone 1 with steady easy spinning on flat terrain.	30–45 minutes in Zone 1 with steady easy spinning on flat terrain.	30–45 minutes in Zone 1 with steady easy spinning on flat terrain.
Week six	30–45 minutes in Zone 1 with steady easy spinning on flat terrain.	30–45 minutes in Zone 1 with steady easy spinning on flat terrain.	30–45 minutes in Zone 1 with steady easy spinning on flat terrain.
Week seven	30–45 minutes in Zone 1 with steady easy spinning on flat terrain.	30–45 minutes in Zone 1 with steady easy spinning on flat terrain.	30–45 minutes in Zone 1 with steady easy spinning on flat terrain.

Thursday	Friday	Saturday	Sunday
2 hours in Zone 2 with 3 PowerIntervals of 3 minutes with 3 minutes recovery between.	30–45 minutes in Zone 1 with steady easy spinning on flat terrain.	2-hour fast-paced group ride over varied terrain; constantly changing pace.	2-hour endurance ride over hilly terrain, staying in Zones 2 and 3 and keeping pace moderate to easy.
2 hours in Zone 2 with 3 PowerIntervals of 3 minutes with 3 minutes recovery between.	30–45 minutes in Zone 1 with steady easy spinning on flat terrain.	2-hour fast-paced group ride over varied terrain; constantly changing pace.	2½-hour endurance ride over hilly terrain, staying in Zones 2 and 3 and keeping pace moderate to easy.
2 hours in Zone 2 with 4 PowerIntervals of 3 minutes with 3 minutes recovery between.	30–45 minutes in Zone 1 with steady easy spinning on flat terrain.	2-hour fast-paced group ride over varied terrain; constantly changing pace.	3-hour endurance ride over hilly terrain, staying in Zones 2 and 3 and keeping pace moderate to easy.
30–45 minutes in Zone 1; recovery ride.	60 minutes in Zone 2 with 4 FlatSprints of 10 seconds each with full 5–10 minutes recovery between sprints.	2-hour fast-paced group ride over varied terrain; constantly changing pace.	2½-hour endurance ride over hilly terrain, staying in Zones 2 and 3 and keeping pace moderate to easy.
2 hours in Zone 2 with 4 PowerIntervals of 3 minutes with 3 minutes recovery between.	30–45 minutes in Zone 1 with steady easy spinning on flat terrain.	2-hour fast-paced group ride over varied terrain; constantly changing pace.	2½-hour endurance ride over hilly terrain, staying in Zones 2 and 3 and keeping pace moderate to easy.
2 hours in Zone 2 with 5 PowerIntervals of 3 minutes with 3 minutes recovery between.	30–45 minutes in Zone 1 with steady easy spinning on flat terrain.	2-hour fast-paced group ride over varied terrain; constantly changing pace.	3-hour endurance ride over hilly terrain, staying in Zones 2 and 3 and keeping pace moderate to easy.
2 hours in Zone 2 with 5 PowerIntervals of 3 minutes with 3 minutes recovery between.	30–45 minutes in Zone 1 with steady easy spinning on flat terrain.	2-hour fast-paced group ride over varied terrain; constantly changing pace.	3½-hour endurance ride over hilly terrain, staying in Zones 2 and 3 and keeping pace moderate to easy.

8

Training Techniques and Workouts

Want to become a better climber? Concentrate on climbing. Want to develop a faster sprint? Focus on sprinting.

It sounds deceptively simple, but all too often, training programs for competitive cyclists try to address so many different elements that they end up resembling Hungarian goulash. Take, for example, this common routine.

Monday: Easy ride, light spinning
Tuesday: Sprint intervals
Wednesday: Climbing intervals
Thursday: Time trialing
Friday: Easy ride, light spinning
Saturday and Sunday: Race or long group ride

Such a varied weekly program will get you fit in a general sense, and it holds plenty of variety to keep you motivated if you cycle primarily for fitness and recreation. But if you want to race—or just see clear improvements in a certain discipline—this approach is too helter-skelter to be of benefit. Imagine painting just one wall in your bedroom, then painting one wall in your bathroom, then the ceiling in the hallway—then going back to the bedroom to paint another wall. Talk about messy and inefficient!

Similarly, by skittering from sprinting to climbing to time trialing, no skill will be fully developed because none receives con-

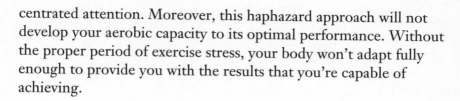

centrated attention. Moreover, this haphazard approach will not develop your aerobic capacity to its optimal performance. Without the proper period of exercise stress, your body won't adapt fully enough to provide you with the results that you're capable of achieving.

The Secret Is Simplicity

The key to improving a particular cycling skill is to focus on it for a 4-week training block—then move, in sequence, to the next skill, and the next, throughout the course of your training year. This approach, called periodization, was developed for athletes in Eastern Europe during the Cold War years. Periodization puts enough stress on the muscles and supporting tissue involved in each skill to help a cyclist gain specific physiological adaptations. An added benefit—one that's especially attractive to cyclists with hectic personal and work lives—is that periodization keeps your training program bone simple and easy to follow.

After Lance completed a racing trip to northern Italy in the spring of 1991 as a member of the U.S. Cycling Federation national team, Chris started the squad on a periodization plan. They focused on sprinting for a 4-week period, then shifted to time trial workouts, then climbing workouts, then tempo workouts. In a nutshell, they focused on one thing at a time. They did it very well. Then they moved on. The team results of this approach speak for themselves.

Of course, you won't become a champion climber or sprinter in 4 weeks. But by concentrating your efforts through periodization, you'll gain the confidence that comes with noticeable, progressive improvements, building on each other both over the course of the season and over the years of your riding.

The Overload Principle

The simple concept behind training is that if you don't push your body to the limit while you're training, it won't respond as it should when you want it to perform. Whether your goal is to ride a century comfortably under 6 hours, to pedal a faster time trial, to get a top-three race finish, or to hammer that smart aleck on your next club ride, you need to overload your body on occasion—push it beyond its normal limits—to help your muscles grow stronger and make your energy systems more efficient.

Old-school trainers once referred to these overloads as shocking the body. And while they may feel like a shock at first, you can be sure that the rewards are worth the discomfort.

How you conduct your workouts depends on your goal. A cyclist who typically rides 50 miles on the weekend but wants to increase his endurance may boost his weekend mileage to 100 miles for an overload workout, for instance. Someone who normally averages 17 mph but wants to get faster would increase his speed to 20 mph on an individual effort. The following tips can help you get the most out of your training.

Recover longer. For overload training to work, you need to give your muscles and energy systems time to rebuild from the stress they've endured as you push them with faster and longer efforts. This means more recovery time. The rides following overload training should be 30 minutes to 2 hours at an easy pace, in a light gear, and on flat terrain (if you must go up a hill, slow down and shift gears to keep the resistance low). This kind of active recovery hastens the process of repair and regeneration of muscle tissues by stimulating circulation to carry away lactic acid and other metabolic waste. (For more information, see Recovery on page 92.)

Tailor your efforts. It's a simple concept, but one that many riders miss—overload the training in the area you want to improve. If you want to get faster, add speed intervals to your training. If you want more long-distance endurance, tack on the miles. Or introduce an element of both to meet your needs. A performance cyclist who doesn't have time to ride more than 4 days a week because of a busy job and family life but who still wants to ride a special weekend fund-raiser century under 6 hours could introduce speed workouts once a week or stretch a weekend ride to double what he normally rides, depending on how riding fits into his schedule in a given week.

Be progressive. Overload training will make you stronger and faster, so you will need to adjust your regular workouts to keep up with your progress. As you make gains in strength and speed, try increasing the number of intervals in your workout, reducing the rest between intervals, increasing the length of the interval, or raising the intensity of intervals to keep your training in a forward progression. As teenagers on the U.S. Cycling Federation national junior team, Lance and George Hincapie used to ride 40 to 60 miles for their endurance rides. When they were training for the Tour de France together, their endurance rides ranged from 80 to 140 miles. Now *that's* progress.

Expanding Your Repertoire

Once you complete one or more of the Carmichael Training System programs, you may want to further expand your cycling workouts to gain a more powerful pedal stroke, increase your lactate threshold, maximize in-saddle efforts, or develop more cycling-specific strength. With the Carmichael Training System workouts that follow, you have all the tools you need to personalize your own training program and focus your efforts to get the results you want.

Remember, don't add too many new exercises to your workouts too quickly if you are looking to concentrate on certain goals. If you want to work specifically on hill climbs and sprinting, turn to Climbing on page 181 and Sprinting on page 195. There are additional Carmichael Training System programs with exercises that will build up your speed and endurance in both of those areas.

EnduranceMiles™

Goal: Increase aerobic endurance for greater stamina

Where: A relatively flat stretch of road with some hill climbs

How: Gear choice should be moderate to allow a pedal cadence of 85 to 95 rpm. Use your gearing to maintain cadence during hill climbs to remain in saddle.

The idea of this workout is to train at under 90 percent of your MSHR in order to stay aerobic so you don't accumulate lactic acid within your muscles, which causes fatigue and reduces recovery time. You should expect to do this workout year-round and incorporate other workouts, such as Stomps or PowerIntervals, into this ride. Ninety-five percent of your ride should be within your Range, however. This is a continuous-effort ride, without interruption.

Training Zones

Ranges	% MSHR	% FT Average Power	Description
1	50–70	30–50	Easy riding, recovery training
2	50–91	45–73	Endurance base training
3	88–90	81–85	Aerobic capacity training
4	92–94	85–90	Lactate threshold training
5	94+	90+	Maximum aerobic training, increasing max VO_2

Sample Workout

★ Total Ride: 60 to 300 minutes in the middle to upper Range 2

★ Begin your ride with 60 minutes in the middle of Range 2.

★ Every 2 weeks, increase your ride time by 15 minutes until you can work up to 5 straight hours of continuous cycling for your endurance cycling workout.

OneLegged™ Intervals

Goal: Isolate the pedaling action for a smoother, more efficient spin

Where: Most effective when performed on an indoor trainer

How: Clip one foot into the pedal. Prop the other foot on a solid footrest, making sure it's clearly out of the path of the other pedal and crankarm. (You can get similar benefits while on the road simply by relaxing one leg and concentrating power from the other leg.)

While pedaling, visualize trying to scrape mud off your shoes—pull your toes through the bottom of the pedal stroke. Simultaneously, at the top of the pedal stroke with the other foot, begin to push your pedal forward just before you reach top dead center.

Caution: This workout is done at moderate intensity—don't try to pedal too hard or you could injure your knees.

Sample Workout

★ Total ride time: 60 minutes in Range 2 to Range 3

★ Perform two sets of three intervals, 30 to 60 seconds each, for each leg, alternating legs.

★ Recover for 5 to 7 minutes between each set (not between each interval).

SteadyState_™ Intervals

Goal: Increase your power at lactate threshold

Where: Any relatively uninterrupted road

How: Terrain doesn't matter—long steady climb, rolling hills, flat road—as long as you stay in Range 4 (92–94% MSHR or 85–90% MSP). It is very important to ride and maintain the prescribed training intensity for the entire interval. Pedal cadence is flexible—while climbing, stay within 70 to 80 rpm; on flat terrain, 85 to 95 rpm.

Sample Workout

★ Total ride time: 75 minutes in Range 2

★ Perform two intervals of 20 minutes each in Range 4.

★ Recover for 15 minutes between efforts.

DescendingIntervals_™

Goal: Increase anaerobic power, lactate threshold, and repeatability during short intense efforts

Where: An indoor trainer for better comparison between sessions, or on a relatively flat section of road

How: Gearing should be moderate, but pedal cadence must be high (110+ rpm) during each interval. Attack each interval as hard as possible. Jump out of the saddle and continue to build speed as the interval continues. If you have to, shift into a lighter gear to maintain the cadence, but don't let the intensity drop.

Your heart rate will remain extremely high and you will train your muscles for high power and repeatability. Each interval is shorter than the one before it, but by design, the recovery time between efforts is limited—you won't fully recover between intervals. Heart rate intensity is not prescribed because each interval is at maximum effort.

Sample Workout

★ Total ride time: 75 minutes in Range 2

★ Perform two sets of four consecutive intervals according to this schedule.

120 seconds maximum effort; 120 seconds recovery

90 seconds maximum effort; 90 seconds recovery

60 seconds maximum effort; 60 seconds recovery

30 seconds maximum effort; 30 seconds recovery

★ Recover for 5 minutes between each set.

Stomps™

Goal: Increase power for in-the-saddle efforts

Where: A relatively flat section of road, with a slight tailwind if possible

How: Overall gearing should be as big as 53×12 or 13, depending on your level of development; it should be hard to pedal. Begin each Stomp at a moderate speed (15 to 20 mph). While seated in the saddle, begin stomping the pedals as hard as possible. Concentrate your efforts on smoothly stomping down during the down stroke. Keep your upper body as still as possible and let your legs drive the pedals. Each Stomp should last 15 to 20 seconds, with at least 5 minutes recovery between efforts. This is an anaerobic workout and your heart rate may not have time to respond.

Sample Workout

★ Total ride time: 45 minutes in Range 2

★ Perform three Stomps of 15 to 20 seconds each at maximum effort.

★ Recover for 5 minutes between efforts.

MuscleTension™ Intervals

Goal: Develop cycling-specific strength for climbing

Where: A long, moderate (5 to 8 percent) climb, or on a trainer with your front wheel set on a slight incline, 4 to 6 inches above the horizontal plane, to simulate your climbing position

How: Pedal cadence must be low (50 to 55 rpm) and the heart rate intensity is not important. (Because your legs are moving slowly, your heart rate will be low.) Use large gears (53×12 to 53×15) to produce the low cadence and high muscle tension required. This recruits fast-twitch muscle fibers, primarily in your quadriceps (thigh muscles), which are important during intense climbing efforts.

Take great care to use correct form during these intervals. You'll need strong concentration to keep your upper body motion-less and relaxed and your pedal stroke fluid and circular while you're mashing such big gears.

Sample Workout

★ Total ride time: 60 minutes in Range 2

★ Perform two MuscleTension Intervals of 8 minutes each in Range 3.

★ Recover for 10 minutes between efforts.

SpeedAccelerations™

Goal: Simulate the acceleration demands of a group ride or race

Where: A flat road with a tailwind, or an indoor trainer

How: This workout is composed of sets of sprints in progres-sively higher gears. While rolling along at a pace below 15 mph, jump up out of the saddle. Use your arms to leverage the han-dlebar. Focus on pulling up on the pedals with your hamstrings. You'll spin the gear out quickly, but don't shift—return to the saddle and focus on maintaining high pedal speed. Your upper body and hips should be smooth and steady. Keep your head up as you drive to the end of the sprint.

This workout simulates the gradually increasing speeds of a road race or competitive group ride. By increasing your gearing for each sprint, you are also upping the resistance for each sprint—and gaining greater power output.

Sample Workout

★ Total ride time: 75 minutes in Range 2

★ Perform three sets of three SpeedAccelerations of 15 seconds each, using this gear schedule.

Sprint #1: Very light or easy gear (42×17 or 16)

Sprint #2: Very large or hardest gear (52×17 or 16)

Sprint #3: One or two gears down from hardest setting (52×15 or 14)

★ Recover for 3 to 5 minutes between sprints; allow full recovery between sets.

OverUnder™ Intervals

Goal: Build power at intensities above your lactate threshold
Where: A relatively flat road, or an indoor trainer
How: Gearing should be moderate and pedal cadence high (100+ rpm). Slowly bring your intensity up to lactate threshold heart rate (80 to 85 percent). Maintain this heart rate intensity for 5 minutes, then increase your heart rate intensity to 3 to 5 bpm above your lactate threshold. Hold this intensity for 1 minute, then drop intensity back to your lactate threshold heart rate. Continue this pattern of riding at your lactate threshold, increasing to above lactate threshold and returning to lactate threshold, for 10 to 15 minutes.

OverUnder Intervals build up high levels of lactic acid. Working in this way trains your body to dissipate and buffer lactic acid, increasing your tolerance.

What Would
LANCE Do?

SteadyState Intervals: 15 to 30 minutes repeated two to six times

SteadyState Intervals heart rate: 178 to 180 bpm

MuscleTension Intervals: 20 to 30 minutes repeated two to six times

MuscleTension Intervals heart rate: 152 to 154

Tempo workouts: 2 to 3 hours/40 to 60 miles

Tempo workouts heart rate: 158 to 160 bpm

Endurance rides: 5 to 6 hours/100 to 130 miles

Normally, the Carmichael Training System will limit the length of the interval above lactate threshold to 2 to 3 minutes, while the intervals at lactate threshold are normally 5 to 10 minutes long. Lactate threshold training is very stressful on the body and must be performed with great care. Please follow the recommendations of the Carmichael Training System very closely.

Sample Workout

★ Total ride time: 10 to 20 minutes in Range 4

★ Perform two to four OverUnder Intervals on this schedule:

> 5 to 10 minutes just below lactate threshold

> 2 to 3 minutes above lactate threshold

★ Recover for 10 to 15 minutes between intervals.

Tour de France, Stage 10.

9

Recovery

Train hard, race hard, repeat. For many dedicated cyclists, that's what the cycling season looks like. And that's where many racers make their biggest mistake. They pour all of their energies into training and racing, forgetting that much of their progress comes from how they rest as well as how they ride.

To perform throughout the season at peak levels, your muscles must be able to recover and repair themselves after each hard effort. Obviously, the more quickly they can recover, the better you'll perform. That means putting as much effort into your recovery as you do into your riding. Just as you can condition your body to take a hill faster, you can condition your body to recuperate and come back stronger after being pushed to the limit.

Rides to Rest Your Body

There's no doubt that racing is the best training. Competition leads to tactical improvements and develops your speed, endurance, and power like no other training can. But once you start racing, learning on-the-bike recovery is critical for your success. Maintaining a proper ratio of recovery and training rides between races is necessary to continue to progress in your performance and to avoid stalling out on a plateau, or even worse, overtraining and hurting your performance. Even performance riders who don't compete but enjoy rigorous noontime or weekend rides with a fast group need to combine recovery rides with their spirited perfor-

How Much Recovery Time Do You Need?

If you spend	You need
0 to 6 hrs at aerobic endurance intensity	8 hrs
30 to 60 min at tempo intensity	8 to 10 hrs
75 to 120 min at tempo intensity	24 to 36 hrs
15 to 45 min at lactate threshold	24 hrs
60 to 90 min at lactate threshold	24 to 36 hrs
10 to 30 min above lactate threshold	24 to 36 hrs
45 min or more above lactate threshold	36 to 48 hrs

mances to allow their muscles to rebuild. (See "How Much Recovery Time Do You Need?")

The days between races, or between hard efforts for performance riders, should be filled with riding at a reduced stress load—what are known as regeneration or recovery rides. Although full recovery between efforts varies for each athlete, the concept remains the same: Ride enough to stimulate active recovery but not enough to introduce a training load. This is not the time to increase your training volume; nor should you stay completely off the bike. Instead, take simple rides of a half-hour to 2 hours at a heart rate of 50 to 70 percent of your MSHR and a comfortable pedal speed. This "active recovery" (as opposed to sitting on the couch) will speed regeneration by increasing bloodflow, accelerating the circulation of nutrients, reducing muscle soreness, and relaxing your mind with some quiet time on your bike. How many days of active recovery are enough? Generally, the more time you spend above your lactate threshold, the more time you need to recover. Anyone who spends longer than a half-hour over his lactate threshold, for instance, needs 2 days of easy riding.

If you don't believe that recovery rides work, consider the recovery rides Lance did after winning the April 18, 1996, Fleche-

Wallone classic—where he spent an astonishing 2 hours at or past his lactate threshold during the race. The next day, a Thursday, he rode for 75 minutes. He pedaled a cadence of 75 to 80 rpm and maintained an average heart rate of an easy 112 beats per minute.

On Friday, he rode for 60 minutes at the same cadence, with an average heart rate of 115 beats per minute. On Saturday, he eased back into some exertion, with a 2-hour ride that included two brisk efforts of 5 minutes each, 2 minutes apart, with his heart rate at 178 to 183 beats per minute. The rest of the ride was at a moderate rate, with an average heart rate of 118 beats per minute.

Those 3 days of riding helped to speed recovery from his effort of nearly 5 hours at Fleche-Wallone. He was able to go into Liège-Bastogne-Liège on April 21, rested and ready to race again. This time, he nabbed second place.

"How Much Recovery Time Do You Need?" offers some simple guidelines for planning and establishing the quantity of recovery time to schedule between races and hard workouts. This is only meant to be a starting point. You will have to experiment a bit to find your own optimum ratio.

Total Body Care

Though much of your recovery happens on the bike, regenerative rides are far from the complete recovery picture. What you do when you're off the bike is equally if not more important than

Listen to the COACH

Don't neglect general recovery throughout the season, no matter what your race schedule. Chris recommends 1 week of recovery every month to build your body back up and freshen your mental outlook. For Lance, regeneration week involves 1 to 2 hours daily of easy spinning to give the muscles an opportunity to relax. For most cyclists, active rest could be 30 minutes of easy spinning daily for a week.

taking time for active recovery and easy riding. Lance knows that total body care is essential for winning races. Here's a guide to taking care of yours.

Replenish your fuel stores. The recovery process begins the instant you clip out of your pedals. One top priority is replacing the muscle glycogen (blood sugar) that you've depleted during your efforts. Even though it can take about 20 hours to fully replenish depleted muscles, you can get a jump on the process by consuming carbohydrate-rich foods and drinks within the first 15 to 30 minutes after a hard ride. Research shows that during this window, the enzymes responsible for making glycogen are most active, so you can replenish your stores more quickly during this time.

For even faster recovery, consider adding a little protein to your postride meal as well. Protein stimulates the action of insulin—a hormone that helps transport glucose from the blood to the muscles—so it enhances glycogen replacement. Plus, protein helps repair broken-down muscle tissue, so you'll feel stronger more quickly. For the best results, research suggests that you should eat about 1 gram of protein for every 4 to 7 grams of carbohydrates in your recovery meals. For a 150-pound rider, that means eating about 75 to 100 grams of carbo and 15 to 20 grams of protein. Two to three ounces of lean turkey or roast beef on a whole-wheat bagel, and a piece of fruit, can do the trick.

If you have a hard time tolerating food right off the bike, some of the new-generation sports recovery drinks are specially formulated with the right carbo-protein-calorie combinations for proper recovery.

Drink up. When you ride hard, you sweat hard. That's no secret. Most riders recognize the importance of hydration. What they sometimes forget is that they need more than water to replenish themselves after an exhausting effort. Whenever you sweat, you lose more than just body water. You lose precious minerals called electrolytes, too. Electrolytes such as sodium, magnesium, calcium, and potassium are what your body uses to contract and relax your muscles. When these minerals get out of balance, as they can during vigorous exercise, the result is muscle cramping and fatigue.

Forced Rest:
A Vacation for Regeneration

Nothing throws a wrench into your training like illness or injury. Yet sometimes, this burden can be a gift to a competitive cyclist. Just ask Lance. While he freely admits he would never have taken a year's "vacation" from cycling, his cancer surgeries and chemotherapy forced him to do just that. The clear result: He came back stronger and more determined than ever despite his illness.

On a smaller scale, this can happen for everyone, whether it be a bout with the flu or time off with a cracked collarbone. The important thing is how you handle your downtime and resumed activity. After a forced layoff from training, Chris recommends doubling the amount of time you think you'll need to return to your previous level of conditioning. For example, if you come down with a cold or the flu for 2 weeks, then you should give yourself 3 to 4 weeks to fully recover. In the first couple of weeks back, you should ride easily just to stimulate circulation and enjoy the exercise so that you look forward to doing more. Allow your body to adapt again. If you feel ambitious, you may start adding a short workout in the third week, taking care not to tax your body or muscle groups. Depending on your rate of recovery, you may want to add another workout in the fourth week. Above all, don't rush recovery. When you take your time to build back up is when you come back strong.

In the event of an injury, you can sometimes find alternative workouts like swimming, inline skating, or hiking to help you maintain your fitness without compromising your healing. Just be sure to clear it with your doctor first.

The best way to stay hydrated is to keep from becoming dehydrated in the first place. That means drinking about 8 ounces every 20 minutes during a strenuous ride and carrying a sports drink to sip from for efforts lasting longer than an hour. When you get off the bike following a vigorous session, you should continue to replenish with fruit juices or sports drinks, which can help keep your electrolytes in balance.

As a rule of thumb, you should lose no more than 2 pounds during a hard training effort. To see how you normally do, weigh yourself before and after your next hard ride. If you lose more than 2 pounds, be sure to drink 16 ounces of additional fluid for each extra pound you lost the next time you go out.

Arrest the free radicals. Pushing yourself to the limit is par for the course in winning races and setting personal records, but strenuous exercise is not without potentially damaging side effects. Vigorous efforts increase your production of free radicals—potentially dangerous molecules that can cause muscle soreness and, in some cases, even tissue damage. The key to stopping free radicals in their tracks is getting antioxidants like vitamin C, vitamin E, and beta-carotene. Fortunately, most serious cyclists generally eat enough antioxidant-rich foods like fruits and vegetables to keep their muscles in good repair. But it's always a good idea to have some added insurance. Experts recommend that serious cyclists take supplements containing 200 to 400 IU of vitamin E and 500 to 1,000 milligrams of vitamin C for antioxidant protection.

Sleep it off. The National Sleep Foundation, a nonprofit public education organization in Washington, D.C., recommends 8 hours of shut-eye a night for the average person—a number few of us meet regularly. If you're serious about your training, however, it's time to take that recommendation more seriously. In fact, if you truly hope to excel, you're going to need more.

While you sleep, your body rechannels all the energies usually reserved for performing daily tasks into helping your body repair itself. Needless to say, that repair job requires more work when you're involved in rigorous training. You can expect to need at least 8—but often 10—hours of sleep a night while you're in training. This is especially imperative for junior riders. Studies show that adolescents need a minimum of about 9 hours of sleep a night just for *normal* bodily development, so they should be certain not to skimp on their rest if they're also riding.

Can't fathom squeezing 10 hours of sleep into a night? Do

what Lance and other pro riders do during the season—take naps. Professional cyclists typically siesta between the hours of 3:00 P.M. and 6:00 P.M. to aid their recovery during training. But any additional rest you can fit into your day will help.

Stretches

Riding hard can give you the solid, strong cycling legs you want. But it can also give you the tightness and inflexibility you don't need, unless you're careful to help your muscles recover their flexibility after each ride. Perpetually contracting your muscles in a crouched riding position can cause a gradual loss of muscle elasticity as well as an overall decline in the flexibility of your joints—both of which can seriously hinder your range of motion and pedal power over time. You'll also be more susceptible to strains and pulls. One way to avoid tight muscles, make joints more adaptable, and prevent injuries is to stretch. Lance routinely stretches for 5 to 15 minutes after a ride to relax and maintain his limberness.

The object is to stretch major muscle groups, like your hamstrings and quadriceps, slowly and gently until you feel a mild amount of tightness—but no pain, which indicates that you're overstretching. Hold each stretch for about 20 seconds. As you hold each stretch, you should feel the muscle tension diminish. If it doesn't, then ease off slightly into a more comfortable stretch until it does. Avoid bouncing or jerking while you stretch (like they used to do years ago in gym classes); that can actually activate protective reflexes in your muscles that make them even tighter.

Instead, make your stretching progressive. When you no longer feel tension at a particular point in your stretch, move a slight bit further until you do, then hold it there. Your breathing should be slow, deep, and rhythmic.

Back and Shoulders Lying Extension

Lie on your back on the floor and point your toes. Extend your arms straight above your face, interlocking your fingers, with your palms pointing toward the ceiling.

Keeping your arms straight, slowly lower your hands until they rest on the floor behind the crown of your head. Hold for 20 seconds.

Lower Back Drop Back

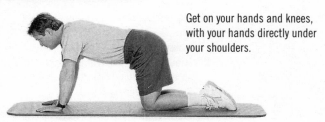

Get on your hands and knees, with your hands directly under your shoulders.

While keeping your hands in place, sit back onto your heels, feeling a stretch along your back. Your arms will be outstretched. Hold for 20 seconds.

Lower Back Lying Back

Lie flat on your back. Pull both knees toward your chest and wrap your arms around the front of your calves, but do not pull on your knees. Pull your thighs toward your chest. Your hips should curl slightly off the floor. Hold for 20 seconds.

Hips Leg Pull

Lie on your back with your legs straight. Interlacing your fingers behind your left lower thigh, pull your left knee toward your chest and hold for 20 seconds. Return to the starting position and repeat with your right leg.

Hips Leg Crossover

Sit on a mat on the floor with your right leg extended straight out in front of you. Cross your left leg over your right leg and place your left foot to the outside of your right knee. Bend your right leg so your foot is tucked next to your butt. Keeping your back straight, gently pull your left leg, below the knee, in toward your chest and shoulder. Switch legs and repeat.

Groin Butterfly

Sit on the floor with your legs bent butterfly-style, with the soles of your feet pressed together. Gently press your knees toward the floor with your hands or elbows. Hold for 20 seconds.

Hamstrings | Sit-Reach

Sit on a mat on the floor with your right foot extended out in front of you and your left leg bent at the knee with your foot behind your butt. Rest your left hand above your right knee; do not press or hold your knee. Keeping your back straight, bend at the hips and slide your right hand forward toward your foot until you feel a slight pull on the back of your leg. Hold this stretch for 10 to 20 seconds. Switch legs and repeat.

Quadriceps | Thigh Pull

Touching a chair or wall for support, bend your left knee and grab your left foot with your left hand. Keeping your knees together, pull your foot up so that your heel presses against your buttocks. Hold for 20 seconds, then repeat with your right leg.

Calves | Step Stretch

Stand on a step with the heel of your left foot protruding over the edge of the step. Drop your left heel below the level of the step until you feel a tug. Hold for 20 seconds, then repeat with your right heel.

10

Strength Training

Cycling is hard on your legs and lower back. But don't think that your upper body isn't getting a workout. You use it to steer and help control the bike. Strength training increases your ability to sprint for a traffic light or push to get over the top of a hill and stay with the group. Since cycling is not a weight-bearing activity (and so does not promote bone strength), strength training is important for overall health and fitness, particularly in older cyclists.

Strength training and cycling don't mix well when done concurrently. The best time to do strength training is during the late autumn and through winter—when most cyclists cut back on their riding because of the weather.

When his racing season concludes in the autumn, Lance heads to the gym for strength training. He considers it vital conditioning for cycling's demands. While preparing to make his post-cancer comeback in 1998, he devoted considerable time to weight lifting. After he won the 1999 Tour de France, he spent more time in the gym than before—his season ended early because of the enormous demands on his time as a result of his victory. He laid a significant foundation for his 2000 season in the gym.

Mandatory Preparations

Before starting a strength program, you have to make some preparations, which will prevent injuries and maximize the benefits of lifting weights.

Listen to
the COACH

Lift lower weights at high repetitions, in the range of 15 to 20 reps, if you want to increase endurance. Lift heavier weights at lower repetitions, in the range of 4 to 10 reps, if you want to increase strength.

★ Wear quality athletic shoes because they create stability during exercise, especially when lifting weights.

★ Wear appropriate clothing so that nothing catches or snags when you're bending over, pushing, or pulling.

★ Maintain proper form throughout strength training. This is critical to receive the most benefit from the exercises and to prevent injuries. If you feel your form deteriorating halfway through a set, stop. It's better to do fewer good reps than many reps with bad form. Avoid jerking and swaying.

★ Exercise with a full range of motion. Don't rush the repetitions.

★ Each exercise set consists of 4 to 20 repetitions. An exercise consists of 3 to 5 sets. Your numbers will vary depending on your fitness and your goals.

★ Always warm up before you begin lifting to start blood circulating in your muscles. Warmups can vary from light spinning on a stationary trainer to calisthenics or stretches. Lance prefers to start at an exercise station and perform a set with light resistance, up to 20 reps to get his blood flowing.

★ Exhale when lifting or pushing the weight. Inhale when bringing it down.

★ Work opposing muscle groups. Muscles work in groups and complement their functions by pushing and pulling one another. Work opposing muscles in sequence, such as exercising the triceps with a pushing exercise and then the biceps with a pulling exercise.

★ Vary the routine. Try 7 to 10 different exercises in a span of 50 to 60 minutes. Depending on the time you have available, do strength training at least 2 or 3 days a week. If you can work out more frequently, exercise one of three muscle groups daily: back, chest, and abs in one workout; legs in a second workout; and arms, neck, and shoulders in the third workout. This allows for alternating muscle groups to recover in between workouts.

★ Cool down with light stretching exercises. Hold each stretch position about 20 seconds, or until the muscle feels like it's beginning to relax. Stretch for 5 to 10 minutes. (For some recommended stretches, see Recovery on page 92.)

★ Cut back dramatically on your weight training during the cycling season. Continue some upper-body exercise to maintain strength.

The Exercises

Although cyclists tend to favor developing lower-body muscles, strengthening the upper body can make cycling easier by increasing power for pulling on the handlebar when accelerating out of the saddle, sprinting, and pedaling uphill. Increased upper-body strength is particularly important to anyone specializing in mountain bike riding, where arms and hands control the bike on rugged terrain.

Shoulders and Neck | Upright Row

This is a good exercise for the trapezius and other muscles in the shoulders. Stand upright, holding a barbell a few inches from the center with both hands, palms facing your body. Extend your arms down in front of you, holding the barbell at upper-thigh level. Your shoulders should be slightly drooped forward, but your back should be erect with a slight forward lean in the lower back.

Lift the barbell straight up, pulling it toward your head until it's no higher than nipple level. Your elbows should be pointing out. Don't sway or rock for momentum. Hold the lift for a count of three, then lower the barbell.

Shoulders and Neck | Shoulder Shrug

Helping to strengthen both shoulders and neck, this particular exercise is a great workout for the trapezius. And since it follows a very natural range of motion, it's very shoulder-friendly.

Stand upright with your arms hanging loosely in front of you. Hold a lightly weighted barbell with your hands about shoulder-width apart, palms facing your body. The barbell should be at about upper-thigh level. Your feet are shoulder-width apart, with your shoulders back but drooped down as far as they naturally will go. Keep your chest out and lower back straight, with a slight forward lean.

Lift the barbell by raising both shoulders to the front of your body. At the highest point, rotate your shoulders toward your ears, then clench your shoulder muscles and roll them toward your back. Do not rotate your shoulders in a full circle.

Shoulders and Neck **Alternating Press with Dumbbells**

Do this while sitting on a weight bench. Grasping two dumbbells, straddle a bench with your legs slightly parted. Your feet should be firmly on the floor, your arms bent. Keep the dumbbells shoulder-width apart at shoulder level, palms facing each other. Keep your shoulders back and your chest out, and put a slight forward lean in your lower back.

Raise the right dumbbell until your arm is straight, but don't lock your elbow. Lower the dumbbell, then repeat with the left arm. Repeat, alternating your reps.

Shoulders and Neck **Side-Lying External Rotation**

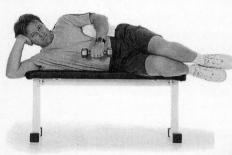

Lie on your right side and prop your head up with your right arm. Place a small rolled-up towel or pillow between your left arm and your body, halfway between your shoulder and elbow. Keep your left arm bent at 90 degrees—your left elbow should be close to your side.

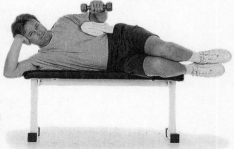

Holding either a light strap-on wrist weight or a light dumbbell, raise your left arm slowly, until your hand points straight up. Lower your arm, then do 10 to 12 repetitions. Do three sets, then switch sides.

Chest | Bench Press

Lie on a bench-press bench with the barbell above your chest. Grasp the barbell with your hands shoulder-width apart or slightly wider. Your palms should be facing your legs, and your feet should be resting flat on the ground. Your back is straight and your butt, shoulders, and head should be against the bench.

Lower the barbell to your chest—right at nipple level. Your elbows should be pointed out while the rest of your body remains in position. Don't arch your back or bounce the bar off your chest. Raise to the starting position and repeat.

Chest | Inclined Bench Press

Lie on an inclined bench-press bench with the barbell above your chest. Grasp the barbell with your hands shoulder-width apart or slightly wider. Your palms should face your legs, and your feet should be on the ground. Your back should be against the bench.

Lower the barbell to your chest, between your shoulders and nipple line. Your elbows should be pointing out, and the rest of your body should stay in proper form. Don't arch your back or bounce the bar off your chest.

Arms Barbell Curl

Stand and grab the barbell so your palms are facing out and are about shoulder-width apart. In the starting position, your arms should be extended so that the barbell will be at about thigh level.

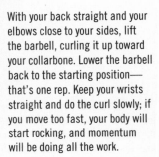

With your back straight and your elbows close to your sides, lift the barbell, curling it up toward your collarbone. Lower the barbell back to the starting position—that's one rep. Keep your wrists straight and do the curl slowly; if you move too fast, your body will start rocking, and momentum will be doing all the work.

Arms Triceps Kickback

To work your triceps, hold a dumbbell in your right hand, palm facing your body. Rest your left knee and hand on a weight bench, then raise the dumbbell toward your chest. Your elbow should be pointing toward the ceiling; your back should be straight.

Straighten your arm out behind you, extending the weight away from your body. Keep extending until you feel the triceps fully contract, then bend your arm and return the weight to your side.

While cyclists tend to be flexible in bending forward, they are notoriously poor at bending backward. Strengthening the lower-back muscles contributes to improved posture and aids in transferring more force to the pedals, especially in seated climbing situations.

Back | Bent-Over Row

To work your upper back, bend over from your waist with your back straight and your hands gripping a barbell palms-down in a wide grip. Your feet are shoulder-width apart. Keep your legs slightly bent and your knees unlocked.

Keeping your back straight, pull the barbell in toward your body so that the bar is touching your lower chest. Your elbows should point up toward the ceiling.

Back | Back Extension

Here's a great all-back exercise, especially for your erector muscles. Position yourself in a back-extension machine with your ankles locked behind the padded bars and your groin area and upper thighs resting on the padded platform. Your hips should be over the edge of the platform, and your body held straight so that it's at a 20-degree angle to the floor. Fold your arms across your chest.

Bend over at your waist, with your upper torso lowered to a point a few inches above perpendicular to the floor. Your arms should still be crossed over your chest and the rest of your body should stay in the starting position. Raise yourself to the starting position, then repeat. Do as many as you comfortably can, working up to no more than three sets of 20 reps.

One of the weakest areas for cyclists (and most people) is abdominal muscles. Abdominals affect the power a cyclist can put on the pedals in sprints, climbing, and time trialing. Weak abdominals contribute to lower-back pain because abdominal muscles balance lower-back muscles.

Strength training here can really pay off, particularly in climbing, sprinting out of the saddle, and preventing lower-back problems.

Abdominals Crunch

Start by lying flat on your back with your hands behind your head or crossed over your chest—never pull up on your neck during a crunch, because you could end up injuring your neck or upper back. Keep your feet flat on the floor and about 6 inches apart. Bend your knees at about a 45-degree angle.

Curl your upper torso up and in toward your knees until your shoulder blades are as high off the ground as you can get them. Only your shoulders should lift—not your lower back. Feel your abs contract, and hold the raise for a second. Lower to the starting position, then continue with your next rep without relaxing in between. As your abs get stronger, you can hold a light weight plate across your chest while you do your crunches.

The pedal stroke is mostly dependent on hip flexion and hip extension, along with knee flexion and extension. The calf does not contribute greatly to the pedal stroke, but some work should be directed here.

Legs **Hamstring Curl**

This simple exercise works the muscle at the back of the upper leg. Using a leg-curl machine, lie with your stomach on the bench and your legs extended out. Hook your ankles behind the lifting pads; your knees should be just over the bench's edge. Hold on to the front of the bench for support. Your toes should be pointed down and there should be some flex in your knees.

Keeping your pelvis pressed against the bench (don't let your hips rise up), slowly and evenly pull both heels toward your butt until your legs are bent at a 90-degree angle, then slowly lower them to the neutral starting position. Avoid jerking your legs up and down or performing these exercises too fast, or you will just be using momentum, not your muscles, to swing through the exercises. Do two sets of 15 raises, resting for 10 seconds in between.

Legs **Leg Press**

To do this exercise, you'll need a leg-press machine—sit in it with your feet on the foot plates in front of you (make sure the seat is adjusted so that your knees are bent at a 90-degree angle or slightly less). Grasp the handlebars at your sides and hold your upper body upright but relaxed.

Push forward on the foot plates and straighten your legs until they're almost fully extended in front of you. Keep your knees slightly flexed—not locked. Your upper body should remain upright and relaxed, and your hands should hold the handlebars for support.

Legs Leg Extension

Sit in an extension machine with your legs behind the padded lifting bars and your hands grasping the bench or the machine's handles (if available) at the sides of your body. Your knees should be bent at 90 degrees or slightly more, with your toes pointing in front of you.

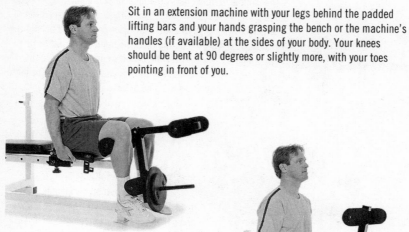

Straighten your legs by lifting with your ankles and contracting your quads. Don't lock your knees at full extension. Your toes should be pointing up and slightly out. To work the muscles even more, do the lift using only one leg at a time.

Legs Heel Raise

To exercise your calf muscles, stand on a box or step 2 to 3 inches off the ground with your feet hip-width apart. Your toes should be resting on the edge and your heels should be hanging over the edge. Hold a wall or a bar for support, or hold your arms loosely at your sides. (If you have hand weights or dumbbells, hold one in each hand, palms facing in.) Lean forward slightly.

Rise all the way up on your toes. Feel the contraction in your calves and pause briefly at the top. Your arms should remain in position even though your body will probably be more upright. Lower and repeat.

The Program

Start with a transition phase, progress to a conditioning phase, follow with a foundation phase, then a strength phase. Conclude in the early spring with on-the-bike power development that helps pull it all together. This way, you'll start the new season with revived interest and greater strength.

Transition Phase

Many racers, including Lance, look forward to this stage after a long racing season. Take up other forms of aerobic training such as running, inline skating, or swimming. Exercises during this transition phase, which lasts 2 to 4 weeks, help prepare your body for the higher intensity that comes later.

Excellent exercises in the transition stage are ones that you can use year-round and involve your own body weight: pushups, pullups, and crunches.

Conditioning Phase

This phase lasts 4 to 6 weeks and stresses light weights with high repetitions. For example, Lance bench-presses 100 pounds at

What Would
LANCE Do?

For my first strength workout after the racing season is over, I use the weight of the bar or machine for the sets and go through the full range of motion for each exercise. I've learned not to dive right back into strength training. Otherwise, my muscles are too sore the next day.

By late winter, after I've been lifting steadily for 3 months, here's what I can do.

Leg press: 400 pounds
Hamstring curl: 80 pounds
Leg extension: 120 pounds
Biceps curl: 50 pounds
Abdominal crunches: 200 pounds per set
Bench press: 125 pounds

15 to 16 repetitions to a set, with three sets in the first workout. He does one workout the first week and adds one more over each of the next 2 weeks.

This stage resembles a rider's long, slow distance mileage typical to spring riding. In both cases, the volume is high and intensity is moderate.

Foundation Phase

This phase lasts 4 to 6 weeks and involves heavier weights and repetitions reduced to a range of 10 to 12. For bench presses, Lance increases his weight to 110 pounds at 10 to 12 repetitions each, for three to five sets per workout.

This phase is similar to adding hill work to training rides.

Strength Phase

This phase lasts 4 to 6 weeks and the workouts continue to increase in weight and decrease in repetitions. Lance bench-presses 120 pounds at 8 to 10 repetitions per set, with five to seven sets per workout.

On-the-Bike Power Development Phase

As the days get longer and winter turns into spring, it's time to turn your attention back to on-the-bike strength training. The key to cycling success is to ride, ride, ride. Take the new strength you gained during the winter and deliver it to the pedals. The OneLegged Intervals, Stomps, and MuscleTension Intervals in Training Techniques and Workouts on page 82 are designed to develop the muscles required for high-power demands that you will face for events.

Don't stop off-bike strength training so early that the benefits disappear by the time your big races or events arrive. A great deal of strength can be maintained with a minimal investment in training by including on-the-bike resistance training indoors at least once a week.

11

Eat for Health and Performance

Before the Ride

Two to 3 days before a big ride or race, your main dietary concern is to ensure you take in a high-carbohydrate diet with plenty of fluids. Lance favors a breakfast with mostly carbohydrate foods, such as cereals or pasta and fruit. For lunch and dinner, he eats bean dishes such as lentil bean stew, rice, pasta of a wide variety, potatoes, vegetables, and meat, such as white-meat chicken or lean steak. Lance avoids fast foods or processed foods.

When the big day finally arrives, eat a meal 3 hours before start time. If it's an early-morning event, get up in time to eat a good breakfast because you'll need the fuel.

Eat a breakfast of complex carbohydrates, such as oatmeal, muesli, pasta, or rice, with some protein. Lance's favorite breakfast before a race or a long training ride is pasta or rice with an egg on top for protein. He usually adds Parmesan cheese over the pasta.

Many cyclists turn to pancakes for breakfast. Chris, however, recommends oatmeal, muesli, pasta, or rice because the syrup that most people pour on their pancakes is too sugary. For those who prefer pancakes, he suggests alternative toppings, including flavored yogurt or fruit such as strawberries, blueberries, or peaches.

About 40 minutes before the ride starts, eat a banana or an

energy bar and drink 8 to 16 ounces (depending on the weather) of a sports drink. This will ensure that you have some fuel in your stomach.

If your ride will last less than an hour, you won't need to eat on the bicycle. You'll have enough glycogen stored in your muscles to carry you through. It's always helpful to take along at least one water bottle. Even on a short ride, it's beneficial to have something to drink to keep your mouth moist and to stay properly hydrated.

Food on the Bike

For a ride of 4 to 6 hours, cyclists typically burn 2,500 to 5,000 calories. A well-trained cyclist like Lance can store 1,600 to 2,000 calories. So on a long ride, he needs to eat to avoid depleting his calories—a condition referred to in cycling as bonking or hitting the wall. An appropriate metaphor, the reference describes what you feel like when you've depleted your carbohydrates.

Symptoms of bonking can include a heavy feeling in the legs, difficulty maintaining pedal cadence, dizziness, severe headache, disorientation, and sometimes hallucination. The remedy is to eat immediately. Look for simple carbohydrates such as energy bars, cookies, or fruit such as bananas. Sports drinks that contain carbohydrates will quickly get into the system—it usually takes about 10 minutes.

Chow down early. Start eating in the first couple of hours, then eat something every hour afterward. Avoid high-fat, high-protein energy bars. Exercising requires carbohydrates, which should be the first ingredient listed on the label. The key is to eat before you feel hungry.

Drink early and often. The same principle applies to staying properly hydrated. The typical person loses up to 96 ounces daily from sweating, urinating, and exhaling. Exercise during hot weather easily doubles or triples that amount. Drink 3 to 4 ounces every 10 minutes during the ride. Carry two full water bottles on your bicycle frame—one on the down tube and the other one on the seat tube.

Grab a sandwich. You may not have access to *panini*, the Italian sandwich rolls that cyclists eat during European races, but you can make something similar. Make a sandwich of turkey and cheese, or use ingredients of your preference. Cut the sandwich into quarters and wrap them individually in foil. The pieces should fit easily into your jersey pockets.

Munch on fruit and bars. Bananas and energy bars are also good to eat, and they're easy to peel or unwrap while pedaling. Experiment with these kinds of foods, however, because they can cause indigestion.

Eat on downhills or on the flats. Don't start to eat while riding up a long hill. The extra effort will interfere with chewing your food.

Keep an eye on iron. Vegetarian cyclists run a risk of depleting their iron stores. Iron is essential for carrying oxygen in red blood cells to exercising muscles. Cyclists lose iron from heavy sweating. Iron is also reduced normally in urine and stool, so if you're a vegetarian cyclist, you need to seek other extra sources of iron, such as whole grains, nuts, dried fruits, spinach, broccoli, and iron supplements.

With exercise increasing demands for protein, vegetarians need to rely on milk, tofu, beans, and nuts. It's possible to be quite healthy and eat only vegetables, fruits, and grains. A strict vegetarian, however, would be wise to consult a nutritionist or dietary specialist. (For more information on postride eating, see Recovery on page 92.)

Coping with Dietary Distress

Discomfort while riding doesn't always involve your muscles and joints. Gastrointestinal distress often intrudes upon rides. Here's how to deal with the common ones.

Heartburn. If you're prone to heartburn, limit your intake of fatty and acidic foods. Also, eat smaller meals but eat more often. Some exercise-induced heartburn can be treated with over-the-counter acid-blocking drugs.

Diarrhea. Return home as quickly as possible and be sure to drink beverages that contain a lot of electrolytes on the way. Treat the symptoms promptly by drinking fluids with electrolytes and taking an over-the-counter medication to ward off dehydration.

Exercise-related diarrhea could be a symptom of an allergy to a sports drink.

Flatulence. This is often caused by overeating or consuming food with high fiber, such as fruit. Reduce the amount of food consumed, cut back on high-fiber food, and stay at the back of the paceline if you want to keep your friends happy.

Eating for Health and Performance

As you assemble a daily diet of foods and drinks that power your workouts and keep you going strong, make sure you find a proper balance of carbohydrates, fat, and protein. When you eat these in the right combinations and at the right times, these nutrients will help repair your body and keep it well-fueled.

Stock Your Muscles with Carbohydrates

A balanced diet for endurance athletes draws 60 to 65 percent of its calories from carbohydrates. This portion of your food intake will serve as your primary fuel source during exercise.

Carbohydrates help regulate fat and protein metabolism and help your nervous system work properly. In addition, your body converts carbohydrates into glucose to meet energy demands and stores the excess in the muscles and liver as glycogen.

It's the availability of this glycogen in your muscles that ultimately determines your ability to function as an athlete. If you're exercising for more than an hour, you'll need to toss back some carbohydrates to maintain your glycogen stores. You can get them from either solid food or a sports drink.

Pick the proper sports drink. Since some people have trouble eating solid food while exercising—particularly during high-intensity workouts—you may do better with a sports drink that contains 6 to 8 percent carbohydrates. This will give you an adequate supply of glucose without slowing the time your stomach needs to pass along its contents. Drinks with a higher concentration of carbos can cause stomach cramps and ultimately hinder your performance.

Recognize the different kinds of carbos. Carbohydrates come in two types: simple and complex. Simple carbos, like sugar, are absorbed quickly. This causes an elevation in blood glucose levels and a surge in insulin, which works to transfer the glucose from the blood to the cells.

On the other hand, complex carbohydrates, like starches, pasta, and bread, are broken down more slowly. They produce a more gradual increase in blood glucose levels. Complex carbohydrates may be a better choice for a longer workout.

Pass on the mushy pasta. Most Americans overcook their pasta, making it too soft. Since soft pasta doesn't require as much digestion, it's broken down faster. Take a tip from the Italians and cook your pasta al dente, or firm. This will slow down the digestive process and allow for a more gradual rise in blood glucose.

A Little Fat Is Okay

Americans are bombarded with diet advice, particularly regarding fat intake. Fat is routinely labeled as an evildoer to be avoided. While it is true that too much fat can be harmful, too little fat can hamper your performance in sports and daily activities.

Fat is an important energy source. It also is an essential component of nerve fibers, and it supports and cushions your internal organs. Your subcutaneous fat layer is important in regulating your body's temperature. And, as your limited store of glycogen becomes depleted during workouts, you must rely on free fatty acids for energy production. This allows you to delay exhaustion and extend your exercise time.

Fat has the unique ability to absorb and retain flavors, which is why it's common in many meals. Rather than avoid it, you simply need to balance your fat intake. Try to limit it to 20 to 25 percent of your daily calories, and stay away from saturated fats, like the kind found in butter, as much as possible. When preparing foods, use vegetable oils like olive and canola oil because they are low in saturated fats.

Repair Your Body with Protein

The remaining 10 to 15 percent of your calories should come from protein. Although it's not a major source of energy, protein is essential for the growth, repair, and maintenance of body tissues.

In addition, hemoglobin, antibodies, enzymes, and many hormones are produced from it. Since most American diets contain ample amounts of protein, you shouldn't need to supplement your intake.

During times of heavy training or racing stress, however, you may need to bump up the proportion of protein in your diet.

Go Slow and Steady to Win the Weight-Loss Chase

As you consider the array of diet information and weight-loss advice that is available, remember the bottom line: You need to take responsibility for yourself and your diet. Maintaining an ideal body weight is the result of a lifestyle change, one that involves improving both your exercise and your dietary habits.

It all boils down to a simple idea: calories in versus calories out. If your goal is to shed pounds, you need to expend more energy than you are taking in. This works best as a gradual process. A sensible goal would be to lose 1 to 2 pounds a week. To do this safely, you need to keep a delicate balance between your training load and your dietary intake.

By reducing your daily intake by 200 to 500 calories, you will be able to lose unwanted body fat, not lean tissue. As part of his preparation for the 1999 Tour de France, Lance adopted a similar program.

Lance Balances Exercising and Eating

In preparation for the Tour, Lance took a new approach to his diet and training. With the event looming, he needed to alter his habits to get ready. Together, Chris and Lance devised a new daily schedule that focused on controlling his weight and maximizing his training time. Lance bought a digital scale and began to weigh all of his food down to the ounce. This allowed him to carefully monitor his diet and provided the information that he and Chris needed to achieve his ideal weight.

A common mistake is skipping breakfast. This puts your body in a caloric deficit and hampers your ability to train properly. To avoid this outcome, Lance would begin each day with a late breakfast. This first meal would center on complex carbohydrates and a small amount of protein. Usually, Lance would have some cereal and some pasta or rice with a touch of olive oil and Parmesan cheese. Sometimes, he would supplement this with a source of protein, usually a couple of soft-boiled eggs.

With this plan, he would have an adequate caloric intake and a good balance of carbohydrates and protein. Lance was always aware of the fat content of his breakfast, so he was careful to avoid heavy creams or fried foods.

After this meal, he'd begin his ride, typically at around 10:30 or 11:00 A.M. He would take a bottle of water and another bottle containing a drink with carbohydrates and electrolytes. During this 4- to 6-hour ride, Lance would carefully monitor his liquid intake to ensure he didn't become dehydrated.

Losing as little as 2 percent of your body weight during a workout can have dramatic effects on your performance as your heart rate and body temperature become elevated. Studies have shown that a loss of 4 to 5 percent body weight can diminish exercise performance by as much as 30 percent. With this in mind, Lance would continue to replace fluids by drinking 4 to 8 ounces every 10 to 15 minutes.

Because he started riding late in the morning, he'd ride through lunch. While still in the saddle, he'd later eat his midday meal in the form of sports drinks and energy bars. By doing this, he was able to maintain his blood glucose levels and continue his training. This system of riding and eating allowed Lance to monitor his caloric intake and achieve his race weight without hampering his training.

After the Workout, More Meals

After the ride, Lance would be sure to provide his body with the fuel it needed to recover. He would consume a mixture of carbohydrates and a smaller amount of protein. This allowed him to replenish his glycogen stores and rebuild muscle protein.

The key is to focus on the first 30 minutes after exercise.

This is commonly known as the glycogen window. During this time, the body has an increased sensitivity to insulin and will facilitate glycogen replacement. Combining carbohydrates with a bit of protein enhances the insulin response and the rate at which glycogen is stored. As discussed earlier, glycogen depletion has been shown to be a major cause of fatigue and exhaustion in endurance events.

On some days, Lance would follow this with a short nap. Over the next 2 to 4 hours, he would continue to take in complex carbohydrates to maximize his glycogen stores and his recovery.

In the evening, Lance's dinner would consist of more complex carbohydrates such as rice, pasta, potatoes, and steamed vegetables. Raw vegetables force the digestive system to work harder, slowing down the absorption rate, so it was important for his vegetables to be steamed or cooked.

By adding adequate protein in the form of lean steak or grilled chicken, he would promote tissue growth and repair, specifically in his muscles. This was particularly critical during this time period because his training volume and intensity were increasing. Consuming protein as part of his evening meal tied in well with the release of human growth hormone, which stimulates the construction of skeletal muscle protein, increases blood glucose levels, and enhances musculoskeletal repairs.

At the end of the day, Lance made sure his nightly sleep schedule complemented the benefits that the proper nutrition was giving his body. In order to maximize his training time, he made sure that he had a solid night's sleep of 9 to 10 hours.

What the Pros Eat

Lance and other elite riders competing in strenuous events such as the 3-week Tour de France require 7,000 calories a day to stay at the top of their game. Ensuring that they eat enough is a job for a small army of support people.

A breakfast for Tour de France riders features pasta and protein, such as risotto and chicken breast. A little protein helps to break down carbohydrates and replenish and maintain carbo-hydrate storage. The pasta is cooked al dente, or just enough to be firm, with extra-virgin olive oil. Lance usually has a little fresh Parmesan cheese grated on it, along with shredded basil. Riders sometimes add an egg over their pasta or a side omelette with chicken or lean steak—no cheese or ham. Breakfast also typically includes toast, fresh juice, fresh fruit, and coffee or café au lait.

Lunch is prepared in advance by the team *soigneur* for riders to carry in the rear pockets of their jerseys to eat on the road. A pro team such as Lance's has a head *soigneur* and three assistant *soigneurs*. They prepare meals early in the morning of the day's stage and then drive out to the designated feed zone. During each stage of 4 to 6 hours, riders also are served meals in musette bags. These are light cloth bags with long straps, which they pick up in designated feed zones on the course.

When the peloton sweeps through, the *soigneurs* stand to the side of the road in their team outfits so their riders can spot them. Cyclists ride past, hold out an arm, and the *soigneur* loops the long strap over the cyclist's arm. That's lunch to go. Riders then transfer the contents of their bags to their rear jersey pockets and fold up the light cloth bags to put in there as well.

Riders eat small sandwiches that typically contain honey and chopped bananas or smoked turkey with a little cream cheese and honey. They also munch energy bars. Then, of course, there's fresh fruit, such as bananas and peeled apples. (The peels can cause upset stomachs from the high fiber content.)

When the day's ride is over, cyclists replenish carbohydrates right away. Within a half-hour of crossing the finish line, they eat baked or boiled potatoes, pasta, rice, or a cereal such as muesli.

In the evening, they eat a bigger meal. Dinner typically con-sists of meat—beef or poultry trimmed of fat—or fish, to provide es-sential iron and amino acids. Dinner includes a lot of pasta, sometimes with roast potatoes containing olive oil, fresh rosemary, and garlic.

During the third and final week of the race, riders need all of their energy reserves, so they cut back on foods that require more energy to digest. They cut back on fresh vegetables such as uncooked broccoli, because anything high in fiber becomes difficult to digest. In the Tour's final week, the cyclists eat lots of pureed food, including potatoes. Most of the fresh vegetables are cooked.

Despite eating 7,000 calories daily, Tour riders lose weight and muscle mass, especially from their upper bodies.

Reach Your Ideal Weight

Many people gain weight over the winter, and Lance is no exception. After the 1998 season, he had gained 12 pounds by the time he started training again on his bicycle for the 1999 Tour de France. Compared to most men his size, 5 feet 10 inches and 170 pounds when he resumed training, he measured on the slim side. His body fat of about 6 percent measured on the low side, compared to the 8 to 12 percent average range for male cyclists and 18 to 21 percent for the average U.S. male. But he didn't want to carry those 12 extra pounds up the Alps and Pyrenees day after day. Like many others, Lance has difficulty losing weight. So he bought a digital scale and every day he weighed all of his food—cereal, bread, pasta, chicken, and lean steak.

He also shifted his training to begin later in the morning, at 11 A.M., so that he rode 6 or 7 hours that went through lunchtime. He returned home between 5:00 P.M. and 6:00 P.M. and drank a protein smoothie for a postride meal. During his May and June regimen, he ate only two meals daily. He stayed on that limited intake even during two weeklong training camps in the Alps and Pyrenees leading up to the Tour.

By the time he arrived in Paris for the Tour's start on July 3, he had gained form, lost the 12 pounds to trim his weight down to 158 pounds, and reduced his body fat to a very lean 3 percent. Riding at a light weight contributed to Lance's success in the mountains, including a victory in the first Alpine stage, which clinched his domination of the Tour.

What's Your Body Mass Index?

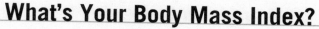

To ride a bicycle comfortably, your objective should be to achieve optimum power-to-weight ratio. The National Institutes of Health has figured a similar measure called body mass index (BMI) to gauge a weight-related risk of developing heart disease, diabetes, and high blood pressure. To calculate your BMI, multiply your weight in pounds by 705, divide that number by your height in inches, and then divide again by your height in inches.

For example, during the 1999 Tour de France, Lance weighed 158 pounds. He stands 5 feet 10 inches, or 70 inches.

$705 \times 158 = 111,390$

$111,390 \div 70 = 1,591.3$

$1,591.3 \div 70 = 22.7$

Scientists at the National Institutes of Health have determined that a BMI under 18.5 is considered very low risk, 18.5 to 24.9 is low risk, 25 to 29.9 is considered overweight and high risk, and 30 or above is considered obese and very high risk.

Lance followed established steps to safe weight loss. It all comes down to balancing intake against what gets burned up. Crash diets are aptly named and should be avoided. Severe food restriction (fasting or low-calorie diets) result in trimming lean body mass and water instead of fat. The best approach is for a slow but steady weight loss while converting fat to muscle for a trimmer body. Here's how Lance lost the 12 pounds.

Focus on weekly weight loss. To lose 1 pound of fat, you need to burn approximately 3,500 calories more than you consume. Reducing or burning 500 calories a day will cut 3,500 calories in 1 week. By doing this for only 2 months, a rider will lose nearly 10 pounds. Shoot for a weekly weight loss of just 1 to 2 pounds. It's not a fast rate but one that is realistic, sustainable, and rewarding.

(continued on page 128)

Lose 10 Pounds in 9 Weeks

If you're carrying too much weight up hills, it's healthier to take pounds off your body than off your bike. Fortunately, this isn't as hard as it seems; it just takes a bit of time.

A Casual Rider is someone who rides 2 to 5 days per week, 40 to 100 miles per week.

A Fast Recreational Rider is someone who rides 3 to 6 times per week, 60 to 150+ miles per week.

This program is for men who weigh 150 to 250 pounds, and women who weigh 120 to 180 pounds. Women who weigh less than 130 should adjust the recommended calorie input so that they consume no less than 1,200 per day in order to avoid nutrient deficiencies.

Week	Eat	Ride
1. Casual Rider	Men: 11 calories per pound per day Women: 9 calories per pound per day	40 miles at 12 mph average
Fast Recreational Rider	Men: 13 calories per pound per day Women: 12 calories per pound per day	65 miles at 15 mph average
2. Casual Rider	Men: 11 calories per pound per day Women: 9 calories per pound per day	Add about 7 miles to last week's mileage; start increasing average speed (about 1 mph jump every 4 weeks)
Fast Recreational Rider	Men: 13 calories per pound per day Women: 12 calories per pound per day	Add about 7 miles to last week's mileage; start increasing average speed
3. Casual Rider	Men: 11 calories per pound per day Women: 9 calories per pound per day	Add about 7 miles to last week's mileage; continue increasing average speed

If your weekly mileage already exceeds the recommended amounts, add 0.5 calorie per pound of body weight per day for every additional 12.5 miles you ride each week.

This plan assumes you're riding a road bike on flat to rolling terrain. If you're stuck with hills, ride the flattest route you can find at the prescribed average to gauge your exertion level, then try to duplicate that when you ride hills. It will involve some guesswork, but it gets close enough to work.

If you ride off-road, forget the suggested speeds. Start by riding for about 4 hours the first week, gradually increasing your riding time to 5 hours by week 5 and 6 hours by week 9.

Week	Eat	Ride
Fast Recreational Rider	Men: 13 calories per pound per day Women: 12 calories per pound per day	Add about 7 miles to last week's mileage; continue increasing average speed
4. Casual Rider	Men: 12 calories per pound per day Women: 10 calories per pound per day	48–55 miles just under 13 mph average
Fast Recreational Rider	Men: 14 calories per pound per day Women: 13 calories per pound per day	72–83 miles just under 16 mph average
5. Casual Rider	Men: 12 calories per pound per day Women: 10 calories per pound per day	Goal: 60 miles at 13 mph average
Fast Recreational Rider	Men: 14 calories per pound per day Women: 13 calories per pound per day	Goal: 90 miles at 16 mph average

(continued)

Lose 10 Pounds in 9 Weeks (cont.)

Week	Eat	Ride
6. Casual Rider	Men: 12 calories per pound per day Women: 10 calories per pound per day	Add about 7 miles to last week's mileage; continue gradual increase of average speed (up to another 1 mph by week 9)
Fast Recreational Rider	Men: 14 calories per pound per day Women: 13 calories per pound per day	Add about 7 miles to last week's mileage; continue gradual increase of average speed
7. Casual Rider	Men: 13 calories per pound per day Women: 11 calories per pound per day	65–70 miles just over 13 mph average
Fast Recreational Rider	Men: 15 calories per pound per day Women: 14 calories per pound per day	102–108 miles just over 16 mph average

Eat smart. For a goal of burning or cutting 500 calories a day, eliminate the first 250 calories by making smart eating choices. Pass up that candy bar or small bag of potato chips and a soda. These extra calories are generally what keep the unwanted weight hanging on.

Ride more. To eliminate the other 250 calories, step up your physical activity. The amount doesn't need to be drastic. Cycling burns up 250 calories when you pedal 8 to 10 mph, so ride an extra half-hour. (See "Lose 10 Pounds in 9 Weeks" on page 126.)

Reduce fat intake. Fat has double the calories of the same amount of carbohydrates and protein. Reaching your ideal body weight typically means reducing the percent of dietary fat you eat. High-fat products include butter, sour cream, mayonnaise, and

Week	Eat	Ride
8. Casual Rider	Men: 13 calories per pound per day Women: 11 calories per pound per day	Add about 7 miles to last week's schedule; continue increasing average speed
Fast Recreational Rider	Men: 15 calories per pound per day Women: 14 calories per pound per day	Add about 7 miles to last week's schedule; continue increasing average speed
9. Casual Rider	Men: 13 calories per pound per day Women: 11 calories per pound per day	Goal: 80–85 miles per week at 14 mph average
Fast Recreational Rider	Men: 15 calories per pound per day Women: 14 calories per pound per day	Goal: 115–125 miles per week at 17 mph average

many salad dressings. Watch out for food with labels that read "fat-free" because that food still may be loaded with calories. Lance's diet limits his amount of fat to the range of 20 to 25 percent of calories, with protein at 10 to 15 percent, and 60 to 65 percent from carbohydrates. For energy bars, he looks for a ratio of 70 to 80 percent carbohydrates, 15 percent fat, and 5 to 10 percent protein.

Indulge your cravings. If you have a sweet tooth, indulge it in moderation once in awhile. The key is moderation. If you don't give in occasionally, you're setting yourself up for a binge.

Keep going. This method of weight loss may seem slow, but it's the safest way to shed pounds without gaining them back. By making small changes in your diet, you can gradually shift to a healthier lifestyle.

Essential Skills

12

The Power
of Pedaling

Of all the aspects of cycling, the one on which Lance has worked most diligently is his pedaling. At once a basic and simple part of riding a bicycle, effective pedaling consists of proper technique and cadence.

Lance drew attention to his pedaling during the 1999 Tour de France's first extended time trial. It was Stage 8, in Metz, an industrial city on the Moselle River in northeast France. Over the 56.5-kilometer course (35.3 miles), with two climbs in the first half and a flat second half, the Metz time trial was considerably longer than the Tour's opening prologue time trial a week earlier of 6.8 kilometers (4.25 miles). Most riders pedaled high gears with a cadence of around 70 rpm. Among them was incumbent world champion time trialist Abraham Olano of Spain. But Lance is a few inches shorter and 30 pounds lighter than Olano, so he didn't have the muscle mass to draw on. Lance found that he benefited from pedaling a lower gear with a more rapid cadence. Instead of pedaling in the customary range of 70 to 90 rpm, he raised his cadence to a range of 100 to 115 rpm. A faster cadence means more demands on the heart and lungs rather than on the muscle strength required for lower cadences in higher gears, but Lance had trained his body for this technique.

Lance won the Metz stage with an average speed of nearly

30 mph. He finished with a large margin of 58 seconds ahead of his rival Alex Zulle of Switzerland. Victory in this stage moved Lance up from fifth place overall to first, based on total elapsed time since the start of the Tour. This put him in the race leader's yellow jersey, which he kept all the way to the finish in Paris. His performance showed that a cyclist can ride faster by pedaling at a higher cadence instead of relying on the power derived from high gears.

It Wasn't Always That Way

When Chris first started coaching Lance, he saw a "masher"—an inexperienced rider who pushes hard on the downstroke while ignoring his upstroke. Lance also favored pushing high gears. Watched from the side, his pedal stroke looked choppy, like he was pedaling in squares.

Pedaling perfect circles is now Lance's goal. By doing so, he gets the most efficient use of his energy with each revolution of the pedals. It involves exerting even force all the way around the pedal stroke, even through the two dead spots at 6 and 12 o'clock.

Soon after becoming his coach, Chris started Lance on a program of drills (which he still does) to improve his pedaling. A good time to incorporate pedaling workouts is after the competitive season ends. During the racing season, most people fall into a comfortable cadence range.

When the season ends, Lance devotes 3 months to working on his pedal stroke. He's a firm believer in going back to fundamentals in the off-season. Here are the drills that Lance uses.

Perfect circles. Pedal through the 6 o'clock position as though pulling your foot back to scrape mud off the bottom of your shoe. Begin the pulling-scraping motion at 3 o'clock. To get through the 12 o'clock dead spot, pedal as though standing on a barrel and pushing it with your feet. Start the pressure at 10 o'clock and keep rolling over the top to 3 o'clock.

Low-gear downhills. During a descent, select a low gear that offers slight resistance as you increase your cadence to 130 to 150 rpm. Avoid bouncing in the saddle, and focus on keeping your hips from rocking around the saddle. This really boosts quality pedal mechanics by helping muscles learn to pedal through the critical

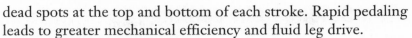

dead spots at the top and bottom of each stroke. Rapid pedaling leads to greater mechanical efficiency and fluid leg drive.

Granny-gear sprints. These are similar to low-gear downhills, except that the drills are done on a flat stretch of road. Shift to your lowest gear (the granny gear), increase your cadence to 130 to 150 rpm, and sprint for 20 to 30 seconds. Avoid bouncing in the saddle and focus on keeping your hips from rocking around the saddle.

One-legged cycling. This drill is best done on a stationary trainer. Simply by applying force with one leg and letting the other leg "go along for the ride," you develop the ability to pedal evenly throughout the entire pedal stroke. Clip one foot to the pedal, place the other foot on the rear of the stationary trainer stand, and pedal in a low gear. This drill forces you to pedal more evenly all the way around the pedal stroke.

Fixed-gear riding. Fixed-gear bikes are found on track-racing road bikes and are designed in such a way that you must always pedal; it's impossible to coast. If you have access to a fixed-gear bike, take advantage of it. This kind of bike is great for cleaning up your pedaling mechanics because it carries your legs through the entire pedal circle.

One-legged cycling drills help develop your ability to pedal evenly throughout the entire pedal stroke.

The Science of Pedaling

Chris started coaching Lance at the U.S. Cycling Federation when the U.S. Olympic Training Center's Sport Science and Technology Division Biomechanics Service program began using biomechanics testing that accurately qualifies performance. In 1991, the biomechanics service introduced dual-piezoelectric force pedals, which were developed at UCLA. These high-tech pedals measure forces applied on the pedal surface, side-to-side and fore-aft directions, and any torque developed between the cycling shoe and the pedal. Special computer software was developed at the USOTC to provide rapid feedback of critical pedaling technique variables for the national team members, including Lance.

The high-tech pedals revealed that the concept of pulling up on the pedals isn't as effective as long believed. The reason is because the opposite leg's downstroke is much more powerful and lifts the other leg during the upstroke.

"Tests on elite riders pedaling at 100 rpm clearly show that most of the power delivered to the pedals arrives during the first half of the pedal stroke, the downstroke," says Jeffrey P. Broker, Ph.D., sport biomechanist at the U.S. Olympic Training Center. "During a large portion of the upstroke, applied forces act in opposition to the direction of crank rotation—that is, the forces are directed downward while the pedal is rising."

The Best Cadence

The other factor in efficient pedaling is cadence, which is the number of times during 1 minute that a pedal stroke is completed. For many riders, going faster is associated with shifting into a higher gear. This doesn't necessarily equate to more speed because higher gears are harder for the legs to turn over. Although it may seem counterintuitive, most cyclists can go faster—and ride more comfortably—by increasing their pedaling cadences rather than going for higher gears. Lance demonstrated the benefit of faster cadence over high gears in the Metz time trial. Lance demonstrated the benefit of faster cadence over high gears in the Metz time trial

Scientific measurements thus ran counter to the concept of actually pedaling perfect circles. Yet data confirmed that when a cyclist looks like he is pedaling a perfect circle, he does indeed have as even a distribution of force around the pedal as he appears. Among those who looked like they pedaled perfect circles and whose tests confirmed that they approached perfect was Rebecca Twigg, six-time world champion pursuit rider on the track.

Measurements of pedaling when computed on clock diagrams show peak power curves when the right and left pedals are near horizontal (3 o'clock and 9 o'clock), Dr. Broker says. Conversely, the two weakest power points take place when the cranks are near vertical (12 and 6 o'clock).

"Lance measured poorly in pedal mechanics early in his career," Dr. Broker says. "He wouldn't get any force going until after the top dead center and only applied it to near the bottom dead center."

The technology helped Lance identify his pedaling weaknesses. Each year, when the season concluded, he returned to the fundamentals to improve his pedal mechanics and cadence. That helped make him a world champion.

and continued to use this high-cadence pedaling style to win 11 of the 19 time trials during his seven-year Tour de France reign.

Tall riders like Abraham Olano and Jan Ullrich, lean but solidly muscled, tend to feel more comfortable at lower pedal cadences such as 70 to 80 rpm. One reason is that the larger the muscle, the more tension it can take, which translates into being able to push higher gears. Lightly muscled cyclists feel comfortable riding at higher pedal cadences because they don't have as much muscle to take the pressure.

The only drawback to increasing cadence is that pedaling faster exerts more demand for blood and oxygen to the muscles.

Lance devoted many months to pedaling progressively faster in lower gears to make his body adapt and balance the aerobic energy costs with producing more power.

After Lance illustrated how fast he could go with a higher cadence, many riders tried to emulate his style with varying results. Ullrich, who won the Tour de France in 1997 and then tried unsuccessfully to beat Lance Armstrong throughout his Tour reign, tried increasing his pedal speed in both time trials and long mountain climbs but eventually went back to his old style. He was better suited to a pushing a bigger gear at a lower cadence because his height and giant leg muscles gave him more leverage.

Overall, there is no single best cadence. Terrain, wind conditions, and whether you're riding solo or in a group all influence your pedaling. You need to work well in a range of cadences. Most cyclists usually find efficient riding in a cadence range of 70 to 80 rpm. More experienced riders usually are comfortable in the range of 80 to 90 rpm.

Mountain Bikers: Kings of the Stroke

Among elite cyclists tested at the U.S. Olympic Training Center, mountain bikers had the most efficient pedal strokes. They applied the best pedaling mechanics all the way around the pedal circle, especially before the top dead center and bottom dead center. Mountain bike athletes as a group rated better than track riders, who had long been considered model pedalers because of their regimen of pedaling fixed gears.

Sport biomechanist Jeffrey P. Broker, Ph.D., of the U.S. Olympic Training Center, who conducted the tests, reasoned that the mountain bikers learned better technique from remaining in the saddle while pedaling up steep mountain trails. To avoid losing traction on gravelly or loose surfaces, mountain bikers apply force evenly on the pedals around the pedal circle.

Lance studied the mountain biker style of remaining in the saddle and applying pressure evenly. He adapted the style to help him ride up the long, steep Alps and Pyrenees during the Tour de France.

Listen to the **COACH**

If your cyclecomputer lacks a cadence function, you can calculate rpm manually. Count the revolutions of one leg timed over a 15-second interval and multiply by four for the revolutions per minute.

Set your cadence on a course. Ride two or three time trial efforts and use different cadences and gears each time to determine which one produces the fastest time. As you improve your pedaling technique, raise your pedal cadence.

Attack hills. A common mistake among many cyclists is to stay in the same gear when climbing, thus lowering the cadence rate. When riding a hill, shift down to keep your cadence to near 80 rpm. Settle into a rhythm to spin up and over the hill.

Keep spinning on the downside. Instead of resting on descents, shift up as appropriate to maintain your cadence rate and increase your speed.

Pick it up when in a group. Group riding usually requires a faster cadence to better cope with frequent changes in speed.

Train for competition. If you're preparing for criterium races, your cadence needs to be fairly quick—100 to 110 rpm. The competition involves lots of sudden accelerations, so you need to vary your cadence paces in training to meet the demands inherent to this type of competition.

13

Shifting and Braking

Chris entered cycling in the era of 10-speed bicycles that he shifted with levers on the down tube. He moved them by feeling the friction of cable tension as the chain shifted from one gear to the next. Sometimes, he overdid it and accidentally shifted two gears—a common occurrence in the peloton.

In 1984, he was among the first to take advantage of the new index shifting that Shimano introduced. These new shifters clicked decisively into place for faster and more reliable gear changes. Five years later, Lance's arrival at the U.S. Cycling Federation coincided with Shimano's introduction of integrated shift/brake levers and eight-cog cassettes, which opened the field to 16-speed bicycles. Then followed nine-cog cassettes for 18-speeds. With triple chainrings popular in mountain biking and catching on with some road riders, cyclists are now riding machines with up to 27 speeds.

While cassettes have gone through a metamorphosis, bicycles remain equipped with two handbrakes. Here's how to use these shifting and braking tools.

Shifting

For competitive cyclists, shifting gears is so crucial that it can determine who wins or loses. The head mechanic of the U.S. Postal Service Pro Cycling Team, Julien DeVriese, who served as mechanic to Tour de France champions Eddy Merckx and Greg LeMond, was so meticulous about Lance's bicycle during the 1999

Listen to
the **COACH**

Watch out for "cross-chain gears," which strain the chain at odd angles between the front chainring and the rear cogs. An example is when the chain is on the big front ring and large rear sprocket, or when the chain is on the small front ring and the small rear sprocket.

Because the chain has the most working parts on the bicycle, any drag or resistance should be minimized. The straighter the chain's line when pulling around the front chainring and rear sprocket, the less lateral tension and drag it will have. When the chain is on the inside (smaller) ring, use the larger-size sprockets that lie closest to the hub to the middle sprocket. Conversely, when the chain is on the outside chainring, keep the chain on the smaller rear sprockets near the derailleur to the middle sprocket.

Tour de France that he slept with it every night in his hotel room. At the end of each long day, after he washed, cleaned, and tuned every component of Lance's 18-speed bicycle, DeVriese took it to his room for safekeeping. He didn't lock it with the other team bicycles and equipment in a secure room in the hotels where they stayed. DeVriese took no chance that someone would mess with Lance's equipment, especially his derailleur. Lance shifted it constantly and relied on it to keep him in the right gear at all times.

A tendency among riders is to ignore the multitude of gears on their bikes and stay in the same one, even though resistance increases as they pedal up hills. Here are some tips to help you maintain your speed and to prevent heavy strain on your legs and knees by shifting like a pro.

Shift early. Shift to a lower gear, which is easier on the legs, at the base of a hill before your speed starts to decrease. You don't want to shift too early because then your legs will spin too fast. Waiting too long to shift will cause you to stress your legs and slow down. Erring either way costs you momentum.

Lance with hands on top of the brake hoods, an ideal position for both braking and shifting.

Shift often. As the hill continues or gets steeper, continue to shift to keep your cadence in the range that is comfortable. By shifting to successively smaller gears, you can break up your workload into manageable chunks.

Listen to the pros. Pay attention to veteran riders and note when they shift gears. In races as well as on group training rides, when Lance goes up a hill, he often hears a tight harmony of clicks as he and others shift at the same point.

Use the wind as a trainer. Treat a headwind like you're going uphill since the resistance is effectively the same. Some of the strongest mountain climbers, including Lance and Eddy Merckx, come from flat areas. They grew accustomed to pedaling against headwinds, and this conditioned their bodies for long climbs.

Don't coast down the other side. Once over the top, shift into a higher gear to maintain speed. For racers like Lance as well as recreational riders, downhills offer the opportunity for leg muscles to recover from the effort of going uphill. To clear your legs of lactic acid built up during the climb, it's best to keep pedaling while going downhill.

Shift up when the wind is behind you. When you encounter a tailwind, shift into a larger gear to take advantage of the assistance. The object is to keep pedaling within a comfortable cadence range. The more you stay in sync with that range, the better you'll feel and perform.

Braking

A common problem among many riders is relying too much on their brakes, particularly when riding in a group or paceline. They are prone to jamming on the brakes to stay in control and seizing the brake levers with a death grip. Here are some ways to put your brakes to work for you.

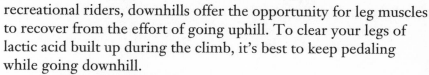

I use my brakes only as a last resort when I need to slow down. I've learned that alternatives to braking reduce the chances of crashing and allow me to lose the least amount of speed. Here are some of my favorite ways to cut speed.

- Coasting. This has the same effect on a bicycle as removing the foot from the gas pedal when driving a car.

- Using wind resistance. I sit up to use my chest and shoulders as a drag. This is especially helpful when riding in a paceline. When I feel my front wheel sliding ahead of the rear wheel in front of me, I slide to the side and briefly move outside the draft protection to blunt my speed.

- Anticipating the need to slow down by looking ahead. This allows me to use nonbraking methods to cut speed as necessary.

Ease up. Gripping the brake levers results in hand and arm fatigue and increases the likelihood that you'll jam on the brakes at the first sign of trouble. Place your fingers on the brake levers, but do so gently.

Develop a light touch. Once you loosen your grip, practice feathering your brakes in an empty parking lot. You'll get used to the feel of your brakes and realize how little pressure is needed to apply the brakes.

Use the front brake with care. The front brake, operated with the left hand, offers the quickest stopping power. But that has to be managed carefully. Relying on the front brake can cause swerving and loss of control, especially in wet conditions.

Tap into the rear's power. The rear brake offers a good drag and is perfect for use on a downhill curve. For best results, feather both the front and rear brakes.

Rain changes nearly everything for a cyclist as water clings to the wheel rims. When you're riding on slick roads, you need to pump both brakes at first to remove as much water film as possible from the brake rims before you use the brakes for slowing. Depending on how softly or hard the rain is falling, coming to a complete stop could take up to 100 yards.

14

Road Hazards

At some point in your cycling life, you're going to crash. It sounds harsh, but it's reality. During the 1995 Tour de France, Lance encountered the worst crash of his career. He tumbled while moving fast in the fifth stage, to Dunkirk in northern France, on the English Channel. The impact of the fall shredded his Motorola Cycling Team uniform. Lance scraped all the parts that made contact with the road—elbows, knees, and hips. As he continued racing over the next few days, the effects of the crash made him feel drained. Staying in the race proved to be a real misery. Nevertheless, he recovered and finished second on Stage 13, to Revel. Two days later, his teammate Fabio Casartelli of Italy was not so fortunate. He succumbed to a fatal crash while descending a mountain in the Pyrenees at 60 mph.

Casartelli's crash had a devastating effect on all of the Tour riders, including Lance. All cyclists acknowledge the risk of crashing, but that doesn't keep them from riding. In a moving tribute to their fallen colleague, the Tour riders rode the next day's Stage 16 in a procession—unprecedented in the Tour's 92-year history—in honor of Casartelli's memory. At the end of the stage, Lance and his remaining five teammates rode to the line together, in front of the peloton. No official results from the stage were listed, and all prize money from the stage was donated to Casartelli's widow and infant son.

Two days later, on Stage 18 to Limoges, Lance made a personal tribute. He rode on a personal mission to commemorate his deceased teammate. He had admired Casartelli for the way he had won the 1992 Barcelona Olympics road race in which Lance himself had finished 14th. On the road to Limoges, Lance rode off the front of the peloton with 10 other riders, then broke away on the final climb to solo for 18 miles. The 10 riders behind chased and kept Lance in sight. When he was hurting, he thought of Casartelli. By the time he reached the finish banner in Limoges, he had a lead of 33 seconds. He had enough time to sit up, raise his arms, point to the sky with both hands, and blow kisses to the heavens. Lance dedicated his stage victory to his fallen teammate.

Staying Upright

Professional riders like Lance appear so relaxed and natural that their bicycles seem to be extensions of their bodies. By the time Lance completed the 2,290-mile Tour de France, he had spent two-thirds of his waking hours on the bike, inches from 150 other riders, for 3 weeks. And he didn't fall once. Part of his success goes back to preventing the conditions that cause crashes.

Take care of your bike. One of the best ways to prevent a fall is to make sure that your tires and the rest of your bicycle are well-maintained and in proper working condition. (See Essential Maintenance and Repair on page 23 for more information on bicycle maintenance.)

Know your route. Being aware of where you're riding can go a long way toward preventing a crash. Each ride should be on a planned route. Try to stay abreast of any changes along the way. Road construction and heavy traffic times are reasons to avoid your regular routes. On regular routes, don't get complacent about conditions. This is especially true in the summer, when cycling and vehicle traffic is heavier and more road crews are out doing repairs. Stay alert for sudden changes.

Chris once rounded a bend in a road he had ridden hundreds of times when suddenly he encountered new asphalt. A road crew had poured it within hours of his arrival, and his bicycle went out from under him in the soft surface.

Listen to the **COACH**

Learn to avoid falls by riding on grassy ground, such as an empty football field, with a friend or two. You'll gain confidence from practicing these drills so that during a group ride or in a race, if someone makes physical contact, you'll know how to handle it. Here's how to practice.

- Ride two or three abreast slowly across a grassy field and bump shoulders gently to get accustomed to the feeling. Get in at least a dozen such bumps, ranging from gentle to rough.

- Ride abreast again and lean against one another's shoulders. Lean briefly and then bring yourself upright. Get used to the feeling of pressing against another rider and straightening up.

- Ride abreast again and bump one another's elbows. Get accustomed to gentle and rough jostling.

- Touching wheels is a common cause of crashes. Ride behind another rider and touch your front wheel to his rear wheel. Pull back, touch again, and pull back. Learn the feeling of touching wheels, and develop reflexes for pulling back when it happens.

Watch out for paint. Lane lines and other painted markers become much more slippery than unpainted blacktop when wet. This is because the plastic paint fills in the pavement's traction-producing irregularities. Avoid leaning through a turn when riding over them.

Stay away from metal. Wet manhole covers and sewer grates are even slicker than wet painted lines. Avoid them by looking ahead and carefully picking your line. Be especially careful on metal bridge surfaces and railroad tracks. Rain makes them as slick as ice. Sometimes, it's better to dismount and walk over them.

Keep an eye on the weather. When it rains, pavement surfaces are slickest in the first hour as a result of rainwater mixing with oily residue from traffic. Concrete is more slick than asphalt. After rain has fallen for a couple of hours, the road surface is usually better for riding. Wet leaves are very slippery, too, so beware in autumn.

Beware of small things. During a Tour DuPont in the mid-1990s, some riders ahead of Lance went down when their front wheels caught in the small spaces on a steel-grated bridge. Bridges like that were designed for motor vehicles, not bicycles. Dismounting and walking across them is usually the best option.

Brake sooner. Water reduces the brake pads' friction on the rims. Apply the brakes to both wheels well before you need to slow or stop so that the moisture is squeezed away. As soon as it is, the brakes may suddenly grab. Be ready to lighten your grip, or you may skid.

Help others see you. Rain and mist reduce motorists' vision, so make yourself visible by dressing in bright colors. Reflective stripes or piping on your clothing is even better.

When the Inevitable Happens

If you take measures to reduce your risk of crashing, you'll be far ahead of many cyclists who take none. But the time will come when you will go down. For those times, here are some tips to treat injuries and minimize damage to you and your bike.

Rely on your instincts. Some cycling coaches give riders tumbling exercises to practice during the off-season in the belief that learning how to fall will help when the real thing occurs. Chris and Lance don't recommend that road cyclists practice tumbling because crashes happen so fast that reactions are instinctive and don't allow time for thought. When you're in the act of falling, there's not much you can do. Mountain bikers crash at slower speeds, so tumbling practice might improve their reactions.

Take it off. Because falls and road rash are an occupational hazard, Lance shaves his legs. When he gets treatment for road rash, he doesn't have to suffer the pain of hair being torn off along with bandages. Shaved legs are also easier to clean and massage.

Wear a helmet. It's an obvious tip, but well worth repeating. Wear a lightweight hard-shell helmet to protect your head and prevent lacerating your scalp. Also, wear gloves to protect the skin of your hands, especially because you involuntarily throw your hands out, palms down, when falling.

Curl up into a ball. When riding in a group, you can potentially limit the damage to yourself, and possibly prevent others from falling, by making yourself as small as possible on the road. Pull your arms and hands in close to your body and curl up.

Clean up road rash. Cycling surfaces have a nasty way of chewing up your skin when you fall on them at high rates of speed. Abrasions, popularly known as road rash, are wounds that break the skin's protective barrier and open the way for invading bacteria. All abrasions, even the most superficial, can be potential contamination sites. Proper cleaning and dressing is a must.

Clean the wound thoroughly. Remove any foreign particles such as dirt or pebbles. Rinse the wound right away because infection can start in only a few minutes. Pouring a stream of water from a water bottle can do wonders in jetting particles from a wound.

In the case of large abrasions, apply a topical antibiotic ointment held in place by a nonadhesive dressing. Antibiotics, such as Bacitracin, ensure that only skin grows in the wounds. Nonadhesive dressings include tape or a fishnet sleeve for arms or legs. These products are usually available at your local drugstore. Clean wounds and change dressings at least twice daily.

High-tech first-aid dressings containing a hydrogel with a 96-percent water solution wrapped in porous plastic are now commercially available under the brand names of Tegaderm, DuoDerm, Second Skin, and Bioclusive.

Turn to RICE for sprains and strains. After the ride, the best treatment for muscle aches and pains is rest, ice, compression, and elevation (easily remembered by the acronym RICE).

★ Rest. Healing takes a lot of energy. Reduce your training to allow for recovery.

★ Ice. To help reduce swelling of body parts that took the weight of a fall, apply ice.

★ Compression. Put ice cubes in a cloth or bandage wrap to serve as a cold compress and apply on the sore area. The ice compress substantially limits swelling. Apply the compress on the injury for 10 to 15 minutes but not so long that the cold causes pain. Repeat after each workout, and two other times at least 2 hours apart during the day, until the inflammation subsides.

★ Elevate. Elevate swollen parts as needed to reduce the bloodflow.

15

Group Riding

Every January, Lance and his U.S. Postal Service teammates start training for the upcoming season at a training camp. The camp is based around group rides because the riders have spent the previous 3 months of the off-season training primarily alone. To be successful racers, they need to resharpen their group riding skills.

Lance learned the importance of group riding skills in early 1998 in southern Spain's Ruta del Sol (Route of the Sun). It marked Lance's first race since returning from cancer treatment. He had trained harder than before to arrive at the start of the 5-day event in his best-ever early-season shape. Even though Lance was starting his sixth year as a professional, his 15-month layoff from the peloton gave him a dose of road rust. He hadn't raced since October 1996 and had missed group riding. As the race unfolded and he joined the peloton of some 180 riders who flowed swiftly in a tight pack over winding, narrow mountain and coastal roads, Lance discovered he had lost his edge in the peloton. He was fit, but his riding skills, especially the ability to surge, pedal wheel-to-wheel with others, and draft behind faster riders, weren't back to the elite level.

Group riding skills aren't just for the pros. Cyclists at all levels can benefit from the social and training benefits of riding with others. In nearly every city across America, group rides of dozens of riders each are a year-round tradition. Usually, the group covers the early miles at an easy pace, allowing time to talk

Strong group riding skills are essential to successful racing. Lance is shown here with teammates George Hincapie and Frankie Andreu.

while commuting together across town to roads with less traffic. Out on country roads is where the hard riding takes place.

Etiquette

While the dynamics of different groups vary, they share a common etiquette that is for the safety of everyone.

★ The leader calls out warnings for surface hazards such as holes, glass, and other debris.

★ Group members share information by passing it along verbally to those behind.

★ When approaching intersections and merging traffic, the group moves into a single file. The leader guides the group as a single unit.

★ Approaching stop signs, the leader calls out, "Stopping!" for the group to slow and stop together.

★ Approaching traffic lights, the leader calls out whether to slow and stop or continue going straight through.

★ The group moves across an intersection as a unit when the road is clear. If traffic is heavy, the group breaks into smaller sections and goes across one section at a time. If the road is clear when the group approaches the intersection, the leader calls out, "Clear!" and the group moves through together.

★ On descents, the leader keeps pedaling to minimize the braking of trailing riders.

The Beauty of Drafting

A major component of group riding is drafting, which is when the cyclist in front pushes through the air so that everyone following closely behind benefits from reduced air pressure. Trailing riders exert about 25 percent less energy to keep up the same pace. Popularly known as sitting on a wheel, a sleigh ride, or sucking wheel, drafting acts as a great equalizer, especially on flat roads.

U.S. Postal Service Team drafting during the 2002 Dauphiné Libéré. Here, the team is shown in an echelon, a drafting formation used in a crosswind.

Drafting involves pedaling directly behind another rider. Usually, that involves a margin of about 6 inches to a foot between the lead rider's rear wheel and the following rider's front wheel at a moderate pace of 16 to 20 mph. As the speed increases, the flow of reduced air pressure allows a greater margin. From 30 mph and up, such as downhills, an interval of a bicycle length still gives plenty of draft benefit.

Group Skills

Riding in a group, whether it's a few cyclists or many dozens, requires everyone to ride smoothly and predictably. If they don't, crashes are inevitable.

Stick together. Riding in a group is safer than riding alone when it comes to cycling in traffic. With six or more cyclists together on the road, the group is more visible to motor traffic. Cyclists in a group tend to get more respect from motorists than solo riders. Whether the group is 3 or 75 riders, members should ride as a single unit when mixing with motor traffic.

Avoid swerving. Despite the rule to never overlap another rider's wheel, it's going to happen. If you swerve at that point and touch wheels, the trailing rider is going down. To avoid swerving, go over small obstacles such as bumps that you would normally avoid when alone. Larger objects such as cars and debris require verbal warnings and guidance about what direction to move.

Be predictable around corners. Follow the expected line around corners. Start wide, cut to the apex, then swing wide again.

Prepare for hills. A common faux pas among cyclists is to "drop kick" the person behind you when standing to climb. This occurs because your cadence naturally decreases as you rise from the saddle, causing you to slow down. The rider behind then hits your rear wheel and goes down. To avoid this, shift to the next higher gear before standing to compensate for the slower cadence and to ensure that your bike doesn't move backward relative to the rider behind you.

Make it a double. If traffic is light and the road is wide, groups usually form a double line. Typically, the leaders pull like a locomotive at the front for 15 to 20 seconds, or up to 30 pedal strokes. Then, traffic permitting, the leaders peel off to the left side to let the next pair pull through on the right and take over as new leaders.

The former leaders interrupt their pedaling to break their speed and fall back to the rear of the group—or somewhere in the middle, depending on the size of the group and its dynamics. Seen from the side, the group resembles a moving conveyor belt, with riders swinging off the front and dropping to the back.

Paceline Pointers

A paceline is a group formation in which each rider takes a turn breaking the wind at the front before pulling off, dropping to the rear position, and riding the others' draft until at the front again. The leader creates a lower resistance in the air flowing behind and pulls the others in tow.

Vary the pull length. How long the leader pulls depends on the group's speed. The higher the speed, the shorter the pull. For

U.S. Postal Service Team forms a paceline during Stage 11 of the 1999 Tour. A paceline is a drafting formation used in headwinds or tailwinds. This was useful in protecting Lance's lead in the 1999 Tour de France.

Listen to the **COACH**

Looking over your shoulder is a learned skill like any other. At first, riders tend to drift in the opposite direction when they turn their heads. Some riders remedy that drift by first pointing directly behind them with their left arm/hand (if looking over the left shoulder) and then turning the head to look. It sounds odd, but it really does help you keep on a straight line. You may find that looking under your shoulder/armpit helps, especially if you're on the drops, as you often are in a paceline.

moderate pacelines of 15 to 20 mph, a general rule is to pull for 15 seconds, or 200 to 300 yards, depending on the terrain. As speed increases, cut back a second or two for every mph over 25 mph. For a fast-moving paceline at 35 mph, pulls get down to a range of 4 to 8 seconds.

Don't hog the front. A common mistake among cyclists is to pull too long. This taxes muscles more than necessary and slows the group, which is counter to the purpose of a paceline.

Stay focused. As the leader, focus on holding a straight line by keeping your head up and picking a sight point about 150 yards up the road. If the road curves, look at least far enough on the horizon to stabilize your path. Avoid looking look down because that causes you to make many little corrections that are exaggerated down the length of the paceline.

Drop off. As you come to the end of your pull, briefly look back to see that the traffic is clear. Keep backward glances as short as possible because the tendency is to drift in the opposite direction. Once the road is clear, move about a shoulder's width to the left of the paceline and break your pedal cadence just enough that the next rider comes by on your right.

After you move to the side, drop back as the paceline continues forward. This is also the trickiest part for novices who may swing away too wide after their pull. Stay close to the passing paceline to benefit from wind protection of the other riders moving ahead. Pay attention to the approaching end of the paceline. When you spot the last rider's pedals, start sliding over for a smooth transition.

Go double when going fast. When speed is rapid and pulls are short, the group typically forms a double paceline. The second is the relief line, created as a result of short pulls. Riders should always stay ready to shift into a single file as traffic conditions dictate.

Sit it out. If you're tired, sit out as many turns as necessary by staying at the back. Let riders coming back know that you are resting, and give them space to move in ahead of you.

Look ahead. A common mistake that beginners make is to stare at the rear wheel in front of them, when they should look up the road to plan their movements. Pay attention to what the leader is doing so that you can plan your upcoming actions. If the leader moves to the left to avoid a hole in the road, then you know the next rider and the one behind will move, too.

Handle speed. Invariably, speeds change up and down the paceline because of terrain and wind conditions. When overtaking a rider, shave speed by coasting, sliding outside the wind break, and raising your torso for more drag. To close gaps, quicken your pedaling cadence but take care not to overcompensate while remaining in the draft.

Deal with crosswinds. Crosswinds cause a linear paceline to lose some of its drafting effectiveness. In this instance, it's best to form an echelon, a type of paceline in which the riders angle off behind the leader to get maximum draft in a crosswind. Always ride to the side sheltered from the wind.

Echelons usually are reserved for races when the roads are closed to traffic. But weekend groups may use echelons if they're careful and limit themselves to three riders across, which involves breaking the group into several echelons. When the leader finishes his pull, he moves off the front into the wind. If the wind is blowing from the right, then he would move to the right, and the next person would shuttle his front wheel to the right. Keep pulls short because the wind resistance is greater than usual. Limit pulls to 10 seconds, or 150 to 200 yards.

16

Riding Out the Weather

Professional riders such as Lance treat foul weather as one more challenge in a highly competitive sport. From February through October, the racing calendar continues rain or shine. Instead of being hindered by it, they dress for it and take other appropriate measures. They have to deal with it, or they'll soon be looking for another way to make a living.

You don't have that pressure as a recreational cyclist, but you still need to learn how to handle the elements. If you cycle only on sunny and temperate days, you're really narrowing the potential days for riding. And there will be those rides that start out sunny but soon turn windy and rainy.

Wild weather fluctuations in Lance's first professional race quickly taught him of the need to prepare. His pro debut came in the San Sebastian Classic in Spain, 2 weeks after he competed in the 1992 Barcelona Olympics road race. The 146-mile Classic, held in August, drew the season's best riders, including eventual race winner Raul Alcala of Mexico, Chris's former 7-Eleven teammate. It was the first World Cup event following the Tour de France.

While it would be a romantic notion to say that as a young rookie pro Lance made a big impression, his debut actually rates as the worst performance of his career. Weather played a big factor in

What Would LANCE Do?

No matter where I ride or what time of the year, I like to wear sport sunglasses for both comfort and safety. Eyewear protects my eyes from the sun, wind, rain, and debris, and it keeps my eyes from tearing excessively during rapid descents.

his struggle to finish long after Alcala had won in 6 hours. Lance finished a half-hour later, in 117th place—dead last.

When Lance lined up for the race, the sun blazed over a typical hot and humid August day. But a violent storm blew in during the second half of the race. Hail pounded the riders, high winds buffeted them, and a downpour drenched them. The deluge converted roads into rivers. Descents became treacherous. Dozens of riders fell. World champion Gianni Bugno of Italy spilled and abandoned the race to take comfort in the "broom wagon" bus sweeping the course of stragglers who had quit.

Lance, bucking a fierce headwind, fell so far behind the peloton that he had to fend for himself in city traffic. The driver of the broom wagon repeatedly honked the horn as he grew impatient for Lance to join others who filled the bus so they could hurry to their hotels. By the time Lance crossed the finish line, the road crews had torn down the grandstand bleachers. Barriers to keep spectators from crowding onto the road had been removed and packed away. The course had opened to regular traffic. He was alone, soaked, and so chilled that he felt half-frozen.

One lesson to draw from Lance's experience is that the weather's unpredictability reinforces the time-tested adage among the pros: Always keep a light rain jacket folded in the rear pocket of your jersey in case the weather changes.

Lance learned his lesson that day. Three years after his humiliating pro debut, he returned to the San Sebastian Classic, rode an hour faster, and won, making him the first U.S. rider to ever win a World Cup race.

Heat

No weather condition adversely affects riding performance more than hot weather. Lance takes great care to remain protected from the sun's burning rays, to dress as lightly as possible on and off the bicycle, and to drink enough fluids. Staying hydrated is the most important consideration when the mercury rises.

Lance drinks fluids before a workout or an event, and then as frequently as possible while he's cycling. He carries two water bottles (21 and 28 ounces) on his bicycle frame and sometimes another in a back jersey pocket. During races, he picks up more replacement bottles in the feed zones designated by the race organizers. Teammates who ride support continue to give him more bottles to help keep him as hydrated as possible.

Tests show that during hot weather, cyclists lose up to 2 pounds of fluids per hour. Dehydration can set in quickly if you don't keep drinking. Dehydration leads to thickening of your blood, which leads to a bigger demand on your cardiovascular system. In other words, your heart is doing more work for decreasing returns. This is even more of a factor when riding on an indoor trainer because there's little or no cooling benefit from sweat evaporation.

Tap into alternatives. There are numerous sports drinks on the market that provide needed fluids, electrolytes, and some essential minerals. Drink ones containing a ratio of 4 grams of carbohydrates to 1 gram of protein. Make sure to drink about 16 ounces within a half-hour of starting. Continue drinking during the ride—never wait until you feel thirsty. Try to drink 3 to 4 ounces every 10 minutes.

Strap on a pack. From the world of mountain biking came the innovative hydropack, a backpack that holds a bladder. A plastic tube from the pack to your mouth allows you to take in water or a sports drink while riding.

For hot-weather riding, hydropacks can be filled halfway, set in the freezer overnight, then taken out the next morning and topped off with sports drink or water before the ride. The melting fluid reduces your core temperature as you hydrate.

Weigh yourself. If you are 2 pounds lighter after a hot ride, that means you're down about a quart of liquid. Carry a water bottle around whenever you're not riding and sip from it frequently.

Hot-Weather Gear

Texas summers are notoriously scorching, so Lance gets his workouts in early. He's on the road shortly after first light, or no later than 6:45 A.M.

Going out early also helps minimize the risks and discomfort of pollution brought on by carbon monoxide indigenous to large cities as a result of car exhaust and industrial waste. To reduce your exposure to air pollution, avoid roads that have a lot of truck traffic. Here's what you should wear to protect yourself.

★ Clothes made of a wicking fabric so that sweat moves through it to evaporate. Wear light-colored fabrics to reflect light, rather than absorb it. Fabrics that are closely woven block out more UV rays than loosely woven fabrics.

★ Lightweight socks

★ Sweatbands

★ Sunblock

★ Eyewear

Wind

Many riders regard headwinds as a natural enemy. Yet winds blow most of the year in Lance's hometown of Austin, Texas, and he has learned that they can work to his advantage. During races, headwinds offer a good occasion to attack. They also provide the opportunity in training to work on increasing power by pedaling against added resistance.

Deflect the wind. On windy cold days, wear a jacket or vest with wind-deflecting material such as acrylic or 3M Scotchgard.

What Would
LANCE Do?

For many cyclists, rain means staying indoors. But for me, a rainy day is still a workday. I dress appropriately and train in it.

As with cold-weather riding, I make sure to wear clothing that helps me stay warm. I pull a Lycra rain cover over my helmet, slip booties on my feet, and put gloves on my hands. To protect my eyes from water spray, I put on eyewear with clear lenses. I wear tights on my legs when I'm not racing, and a jacket made of water-repellent fabric.

I look for raingear that breathes to allow my body to stay warm when it's cold and cool when it's hot. I also ensure that my raingear won't get baggy in the rain or get caught in the chain.

Pedal hard while going out. For long rides on windy days, go out against the wind. You'll reap the benefit of a tailwind on your return. Tailwinds offer the opportunity to practice high-speed sprints because the boost simulates riding in a peloton.

Stay indoors. Don't risk riding in severe winds that will blow you off the road or into traffic. At the U.S. Olympic Training Center, winds howl at 60 to 70 mph. On those days, Lance trained indoors or waited for the wind to subside.

Cold

When preparing to ride in cold weather, the best advice is to dress in layers. Dressing in layers allows you to remove your jacket if the weather warms up, such as when the sun emerges from cloud cover, or when you pedal up long hills. When you hit a climb, unzip your top layer. If it's a long climb, you may even want to remove your outer jacket. At the summit, put the outer layer back on. If it's a long descent, put on a rain jacket as well to protect yourself from the windchill on the descent.

Stay at home when ice arrives. When conditions are icy, your chances of crashing go way up, especially in shady areas that may hide slick black ice. Icy days are a good time to either pedal indoors on a stationary trainer or hit the gym.

Ride when it's clear. Pollution problems are usually associated with hot weather. But cold weather can also produce aggravating carbon monoxide levels. The best time to ride is in the afternoon. Mornings typically have light winds, which means pollutants stagnate in the air.

Pull it on when going down. Television audiences following the Tour de France up and down the Alps and Pyrenees saw Lance straighten up on his bicycle when he reached summits. He was reaching back into his jersey pocket to pull out a vest to ward off a chill during high-speed descents. There's no reason the same trick can't work for you.

Recover after a ride. Winter takes more out of you because of the elements and a lower fitness level. Don't ride as long, and allow more recovery time than after warmer rides.

2003 Liège-Bastogne-Liège.

Windchill Chart

Wind (mph)	Temperature (°F)									
0	35	30	25	20	15	10	5	0	-5	-10
	Equivalent Temperature (°F)									
5	32	27	22	16	11	6	0	-5	-10	-15
10	22	16	10	3	-3	-9	-15	-22	-27	-34
15	16	9	2	-5	-11	-18	-25	-31	-38	-45
20	12	4	-3	-10	-17	-24	-31	-39	-46	-53
25	8	1	-7	-15	-22	-29	-36	-44	-51	-59
30	6	-2	-10	-18	-25	-33	-41	-49	-56	-64
35	4	-4	-12	-20	-27	-35	-43	-52	-58	-67
40	3	-5	-13	-21	-29	-37	-45	-53	-60	-69

Cold-Weather Gear

Apparel is now one of the most tech-heavy industries in cycling. Synthetics such as Lycra, polypropylene, and polyester have gone through several generations of improvements for durability. The good thing about these synthetics is that they breathe, which means they absorb moisture and wick it through to the outside of the fabric, where it quickly evaporates to avoid chills or over-heating.

A wide range of outdoor wear helps to keep Lance and other pros pedaling on the roads through all kinds of chilly, windy, and rainy weather. He takes special care to cover his extremities—head, hands, and feet.

You want to dress for a cold-weather ride with enough clothing to feel cool when starting out because your core body temperature will soon rise.

Head. To keep your head warm when the mercury drops below 45°F, pull a cover made of Lycra or Gore-Tex over your helmet. Underneath the helmet, wear cycling-specific headgear because not just any stocking cap fits. Synthetic mixes wick moisture better. Here are some of your options.

★ Balaclavas, which cover the head to the neck, leaving openings for the eyes and mouth. It keeps the head warm while protecting the face from windchill on sub-freezing rides.

★ Beanies made of polyester and spandex fit over the crown of your head and are good for 40°F to 30°F temperatures.

★ Headbands that cover your ears are good for temperatures that range from 48°F to 20°F.

★ Earmuffs with the retention band tucked behind the head rather than under the helmet for temperatures that range from 48°F to 20°F.

Hands. Gloves come in a wide range of styles and weights for different climates and personal preferences. When buying gloves, purchase at least two pairs—a medium-weight pair to take the chill off in weather below 50°F, and a heavier, thicker pair for sub-freezing temperatures. The medium-weight pair are usually the standard five-finger gloves. For cold-weather gloves, you might prefer split-finger (lobster) gloves or mittens.

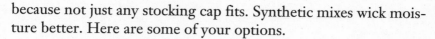

Listen to the COACH

Suffering from a cold and wondering whether to ride? If you have a fever, never go riding or exercise. If you have upper respiratory congestion or mild blockage of the sinuses, mild to moderate exercise may alleviate your symptoms and stimulate your circulation to hasten recovery. One advantage that exercise offers blocked sinuses is that it gets more moisture in them to open them up and help prevent further infections. Take care not to tax your body, however. Stay within a comfortable time span, such as an hour.

Listen to the COACH

In cold weather, equip your wheels with heavier tires than usual to reduce the chances of getting a flat. After all, changing a tire usually means removing gloves. Some roadies even ride their mountain bikes on the road during cold weather because the tires are better able to handle the road grit, salt, ice, and other hazards.

Feet. Booties are available in many styles and weights. Full neoprene booties extend to the bottom of the calf to keep your feet warm for riding from 45°F down to 20°F. Smaller booties that cover only the forefoot protect the feet on days with chilly mornings or damp roads that kick up spray.

Chronically cold feet are often caused by constriction of blood vessels rather than cold air temperature. If you find that your feet are uncomfortably cold while wearing two pairs of socks, you could be wearing footgear that is too tight. Ordinarily, neoprene booties over cycling shoes and Gore-Tex socks are adequate to keep your feet warm down to 20°F.

Legs. Lance likes to wear tights with bib tops to keep them from pulling down during a ride. If the temperature is near freezing or colder, put on a second pair of shorts under the tights to keep warm.

Upper body. Arm warmers can be conveniently removed if the temperature rises enough to allow you to ride in a short-sleeved jersey. Unused warmers can be folded into jersey pockets.

Vests are important in cold weather because your chest gets hit the most by the wind. Vests come in a variety of styles and weights. Usually, they have solid wind-blocking fabric or a mesh liner on the front to protect the chest, a thinner fabric on the back, and three rear pockets that offer more places to carry spare clothes.

Jackets with multilayer membrane fabrics repel wind and rain, retain body heat, and allow the fabric to breathe. You may want to own two or three jackets of varying weights for use in assorted weather conditions.

Techniques to Ride like a Pro

17

Mental Toughness

In 2003 Lance was poised to join an elite club of racers with five Tour de France victories to their credit, but his long streak of good fortune at the Tour seemed to unravel and put number five in jeopardy. The race was held during a heat wave that eventually killed more than 10,000 people in France, Lance took a forced detour through a field to avoid crashing with Joseba Beloki, suffered a dehydration crisis and lost 1:36 to rival Jan Ullrich in the Stage 12 individual time trial, was only 15 seconds in front of Ullrich after the following day, and then crashed on his way up the final climb to the finish of Stage 15.

Through all the adversity, Lance and his teammates stayed in control. The team knew Lance was vulnerable after Stage 12, and even though they were already a close-knit team, they pulled together even more to support their leader over the next three stages through the mountains. When Lance's handlebar snagged a fan's mussette bag and flipped him onto the road to Luz Ardiden, it could have been the final nail in his coffin. His lead over Ullrich was only 15 seconds, and Lance knew that day was his last chance to put some distance between him and the German before the race left the mountains. He and his teammates had been fighting so hard, in the face of severe adversity, for days, but Lance summoned the will to pour everything he had left into leaving Ullrich behind by 40 seconds on that climb. With the time bonus for winning the stage, Lance extended his lead to a more comfortable, but still tenuous 1:07. Six days later, his teammates led him onto the Champs Elysees in Paris as the newest five-time Tour de France winner. On the podium, he dedicated his victory to his teammates. How did Lance and his teammates manage to ride with such panache and exhibit so much mental toughness?

Mental toughness stems from the mind and body working together to achieve goals. The Postal Service team performed like champions by blending mental preparation and setting smart goals with hard, focused physical training. Everyone who achieves success, whether in cycling or any other pursuit, does so because of commitment and passion. The holistic approach of preparing both the mind and body were key to Lance's victories in the Tour, arguably the toughest challenge in the world of sports.

What motivates Lance to race up to 120 days between February and October? He admits that there are many times when he feels he doesn't want to be there. Cold days in relentless rain and penetrating wind, and the constant threat of crashes make harsh conditions for riding a bicycle. But because he has survived cancer and its treatment, he knows that he has endured worse ordeals. This perspective helps him continue and not get discouraged when he's suffering on his bicycle.

To gain an optimistic point of view and eliminate doubt, Lance and his teammates set a series of microgoals each year that led up to the ultimate goal of winning the Tour de France. All of his training and races leading up to the Tour were preparation for those 3 weeks in July. This mental process anchored Lance's desires and commitment to training so that he was able to carry out a yearlong program.

Part of maintaining a fresh outlook day in and day out is taking a break to do other things that engage your interest. When Lance finishes his ride for the day, whether it's a training ride or a Tour de France stage, he'll log onto his computer to surf the Web. He also reads magazines and likes to watch movies. Lance also devotes considerable time and energy to the Lance Armstrong Foundation, a multimillion-dollar foundation in Austin, Texas, devoted to fighting cancer through research, awareness, and education.

Listen to the COACH

I've seen many athletes win World Championships and Olympic and Pan American Games medals while others, equally talented, fall short. What's the critical difference between athletes who succeed and those who go home empty-handed? Those who succeed have blended the mental aspects necessary for success into their physical training programs. When they try to achieve their goals but come up short, they don't see failure. They see that they've found an approach that doesn't work. Instead of quitting, they train differently or refocus to reach their goals.

All champions share the knack of maintaining a strong focus; they can turn it on and off. During the Tour de France, when the French media created chaos over unfounded accusations of Lance's alleged use of banned medications, he kept his thoughts on the Tour—his main rivals, the teams they ride for, upcoming stages, the roads ahead. It would have been easy to let the media distractions overwhelm him. Yet when he had finished riding for the day, he didn't ponder anything negative. Consequently, he went into the final time trial, which he won, with a positive attitude. Those performances also kept up the team's spirits and contributed to their momentum.

Goals to Success

There is no single formula for success in cycling, but there is universal agreement that setting goals is part of any winning formula for achieving success. Before you can chase your desires, you have to figure out exactly what they are and what you need to do to attain them. Is it to ride a century in a certain time? Or to win a local road race? Or is it to lose a certain amount of weight? No matter what the goal, making a plan is a must.

At times, the work involved in fulfilling a goal becomes difficult—the competition seems overwhelming, the weather may be icy and wet, family and work responsibilities increase, or you may

Get Past a Training Plateau

A universal problem among athletes is hitting a plateau in their training and figuring out how to get past it. The holistic approach of addressing both the mental and physical aspects of this problem is the best way to overcome it.

Change. Be receptive to different training and racing approaches. Think of things from a different perspective. Some like to call it breaking the mold, looking at the big picture, or thinking outside the box. Athletes often complain that 2 years ago, they were riding long distances at this time of the year, or they were doing a certain number of sprint intervals, and they would be flying. But now, they can't seem to get any better. Some people think that if a routine worked once, it will work again. But things change, and many factors affect performances.

Walk away from it. If you've been trying to conquer a killer hill at a certain average speed but just can't seem to do it, then take a break from battling the hill. Focus on something else, such as improving your sprinting or your descending skills. Return to the hill several weeks later, and you'll probably be surprised that you can successfully tackle your goal.

Empower yourself. Realize that you control the outcome of your cycling success. Not the weather, not your competitors, not your work. Instead of blaming the rain for not getting in a training ride, set up your stationary trainer and go for a spin. Taking positive control of your cycling program is key to achieving your goals.

---

crash hard. Your commitment to your goal can keep you hanging in there. Realize that the road to a goal can change. Adapt your training to accommodate life's pressures, but always stay focused on the goal.

Add small goals along the way. To avoid straying from the effort required to train for a goal that is months away, focus on a short-term goal of several weeks or a month. This could be anything from competing in a short race to conquering a nearby hill. Limit yourself to two goals per 4-week training period.

Break down workouts. Every workout should have a list of goals attached, such as a certain cadence, heart rate, or mileage. Keep these in mind and every workout will have a built-in element of motivation.

Categorize goals. Place goals into broad groups. One goal could be to lose 10 pounds. Another one could be to improve your lactate threshold. Or you might aspire to improve your group-riding confidence or climbing skills.

Write them down. Cement the goals in your program by writing them down in a log. Then use the log to track your daily progress, which in itself will motivate you to stay on track.

Target a Peak Performance

The maximum intensity in your training program should occur 3 weeks before your targeted peak performance. You've done a lot of work leading up to this point to increase your aerobic capacity, strength, endurance, and skills.

The 3 weeks before the peak event should be devoted to tapering and training specifically for the event. Tapering involves gradually cutting back on your training to rest your muscles and prepare your body both mentally and physically for a peak performance.

What Would
▬▬ LANCE Do?

I generally determine my major goals a year in advance. After winning the 1999 Tour de France, I set two major goals for 2000: to successfully defend my Tour victory and to win a medal at the Summer Olympics in Sydney, Australia. I realize that there are many variables outside of my control in my quest, but focusing on a big goal down the road really motivates me. To help me stay focused, I set microgoals such as races or training achievements that bring me one step closer to being at my best for my major goals. Whatever the final results of my goal events, I can at least look back and say that I gave it my best effort and was prepared.

Reduce the volume. Cut down your total weekly training time by 5 percent to 10 percent 2 weeks in advance of the target event. Then, with 1 week to go, trim your volume by another 5 percent. So if you're routinely riding 15 hours a week, then cut back to 13.5 hours with 2 weeks to go, then to less than 13 hours in the final week before the event.

Check out the course. If possible, ride along the length of the target course and customize your taper training to simulate event conditions. Does it include a lot of hills? If so, then include hill workouts to practice those skills. Is the ride going to be in the heat of the day? If so, then do your workouts in the heat of the day.

Keep up the intensity. If you're a recreational rider, your rides should be challenging but shorter than usual. If you're a racer, training rides should be above race intensity or speed but less than the race distance.

Lance's teammate Dylan Casey competed in the 1999 Pan American Games in Winnipeg, Manitoba, Canada. His event was the individual pursuit, a 4000-meter (2.5 miles) time trial. In the 3 weeks leading up to the PanAm Games, Casey's workouts were intense but short. He rode half his distance, 2 kilometers (1.25 miles), at a pace 3 to 4 seconds faster than his race pace. On race day, Casey scored the cycling team's first gold medal and set a new PanAm Games pursuit record.

Experiment. The more conditioned you are, the less taper you'll need. For the 1999 Tour de France, Lance tapered only 3 days. The only sure way to discover your perfect taper length is to experiment. Starting out as suggested above, however, is a good way to start.

Taper your mind, too. Preparing mentally for a peak performance can be more tricky than preparing your body. Physically, you have your workouts and you can cut exact lengths and distances. It's not as simple with your mind. Concentrate on the goal ahead. Try to block out distractions as you wind down your training. At the same time, visualize success and remind yourself of the hard work you've put into getting ready for this peak event.

Hitting his peak: Lance climbs out of the saddle during Stage 15 of the 1999 Tour de France.

Practice patience. Many cyclists ruin their conditioning in the final stages of peaking simply because they try to fill the hours freed up from reduced training with other activities. Sit back and relax, preparing mentally and physically for your targeted event. Use the time to ensure that your bike is tuned up and ready to go. And make sure you get at least 8 hours of sleep every night.

Stick to the tried and true. Three days before your event is not the time to try a new training technique or food. Stay on track with foods that you like and that agree with you.

Establish a routine. This is important for the night before and throughout the day of the event. An established ritual will better your chances of getting a solid night's rest. Plan the race day back from the race start so that you wake up in plenty of time to get a good breakfast and can get to the site with time to warm up, assemble your bike, and eat a snack. A well-established routine keeps your mind focused.

18

Cornering

Growing up in the warm weather and flat terrain of suburban Dallas, Lance had limited opportunities to develop sound cornering skills. Once he made the U.S. Cycling Federation national team and traveled to races around the world, he faced all kinds of weather conditions and terrain, from winding descents down mountains without any guardrails to rainy, and sometimes snowy, roads.

Lance quickly learned that taking corners on a bicycle, whether racing or riding casually, involves more than just squeezing the brakes and turning the handlebar.

Strategies to Corner like a Pro

While on the approach, set up for taking the corner. Judge the speed you're traveling and what you need to take the corner safely. Ideally, you want to carry as much speed as possible when coming out of the corner. You'll need to make a judgment, based on experience, skill, and the road surface, whether to brake or maintain speed. If slowing is called for, apply the brakes before starting to make the arc for the turn.

In the corner. Keep the inside pedal up at 12 o'clock. This accomplishes two things: First, it prevents the pedal from clipping on the pavement, which could cause a fall as you lean into the corner. Second, it offers the opportunity to apply downward pressure on the opposite pedal, at 6 o'clock, to increase the bicycle's stability. On sweeping turns or at a slow speed around corners, it's possible to pedal all the way through. If you realize you've misjudged the speed for a tight turn and must slow down, use both front and rear brakes simultaneously, rather than just one brake.

If you happen upon a tight corner with too much speed, it is sometimes better to lay off the brakes. When brakes are applied, they make your bicycle track in a straight direction—the harder the braking, the more forcefully the bicycle tracks straight. In these cases, keep your body upright, push your bicycle down, and press the tires onto the road. This technique helped Lance corner during his solo breakaway on rain-slick roads in Oslo to win the 1993 World Championship Road Race.

Out of the corner. Move the bicycle upright and resume pedaling to increase your speed.

One cornering technique is known as the rule of Outside/Inside/Outside. As you approach a corner, check the traffic flow behind you with a brief glance over your shoulder to make sure that the road is clear. If it is, move outside to the edge of your lane. Go through the turn on a tangent inside the corner. After the corner, let your momentum take you outside to the edge of your lane. Then promptly move back to the right side of the road to get out of the way of the traffic flow. This technique should be used only on lightly trafficked roads. If you're riding in traffic, take the corner at a slow enough speed that allows you to remain along the right side of the road at all times.

Lance in the corner, knee turned in and pressed against the top tube, during the 2003 (Stage 19) Tour de France.

What Would
▐ LANCE Do?

There are a number of dangers that a cyclist faces on the road. The most common one, especially when cornering, is a wet or unstable surface, which is often caused by loose sand or gravel. Here are my suggestions for handling slick conditions.

- After rainfall, stay away from the center of the road, where rainwater tends to accumulate.

- Avoid road paint and metal surfaces, especially manhole covers and bridge seams, all of which become slick when wet.

- Brake well in advance of where you would on dry pavement.

- Lower your center of gravity by placing your hands on the drops, bend your elbows, lower your back so that it's parallel to the ground, and slide your butt back over the saddle to put more weight on your rear wheel.

- Corner more slowly, which reduces leaning and thus provides the maximum amount of tire surface for the road.

Remember that just because it hasn't rained doesn't mean that a road isn't slick. Dry roads are prone to being slick in hot weather as a result of high humidity mixing with the film of oil from motor-vehicle traffic—a condition I've encountered often on Texas roads.

Taking a corner at speed. The preferred technique of Lance and the pros is to lean the bicycle instead of the body. You can corner fastest by leaning the bicycle down, pressing it with your hands to keep your body as perpendicular to the ground as possible.

Your outside elbow should be bent while the inside elbow remains straight to stretch out the turn. Your outside foot should be pressed down on the bottom of the stroke, at 6 o'clock, with the outside leg remaining straight, while the inside knee is bent and the inside pedal is up high at 12 o'clock. Once out of the turn, move the bicycle upright as soon as possible to maintain the maximum amount of speed.

Body Placement

The position of your body is very important to mastering corners.

Head. Keep your head perpendicular to the road so that your inner ear can maintain balance. Your eyes should look up the road because you tend to go where your eyes are looking.

Torso. Lower your torso by bending your elbows and sliding your butt back to distribute more weight over the rear of the bicycle. Your back should be parallel with the top tube.

Hands. Move your hands to the drops for maximum control of the bicycle, to gain the best access to the brake levers, and to lower your center of gravity. Depending on your confidence, your skill, and your speed going into the corner, you may also put your hands on the hoods or the top of the handlebar. In any case, position your hands well before the turn. Don't squeeze the handlebar. Firmly hold it to guide, rather than force, the bicycle around the corner.

Arms. Bend your elbows for better aerodynamic position that reduces drag to help carry as much speed as possible through the turn, serve as shock absorbers over any bumps, and lower your torso's center of gravity.

Feet. Set your soles firmly on the pedals to bear weight as you shift on the saddle for balance. Your outside foot takes your weight inside a corner on a tight turn.

Knees. Lance learned the technique of pressing the inside knee against the top tube from his English teammate Sean Yates, who had raced against Chris in Europe in the late 1980s. Chris recalls riding with Sean on climbs in Paris-Nice, trailing the leaders by about 10 minutes on a mountain stage in southern France. Down the winding descents, Sean, one of the tallest riders in the peloton at 6 feet 2 inches, dropped Chris and the group they were in.

Sean perfected his cornering style and passed it on to Lance.

Lance at full speed during Stage 21, the final stage of the 2005 Tour.

Pressing the inside knee against the top tube allows you to keep pressure on the outside pedal through the turn and make the bicycle more stable while leaning the bicycle. Shift your hips a little bit to the outside of the saddle and place more weight on the outside leg. Place your hands on the drops, bend your elbows, and lower your back flat over the top tube.

Another technique is throwing the inside knee out from the top tube, like motorcycle racers. Although it has long been a popular technique, it is not recommended by Chris or Lance because it creates instability.

19

Climbing

By the time the 2001 Tour de France reached the Alps, the world knew about Lance Armstrong's ability to spin up steep climbs at an incredible pace, but he still had a few tricks up his sleeve. On Stage 10, he feigned weakness on the early climbs of the day, giving false hope to his rivals who took the bait and drove the pace to the bottom of the famous switchbacks of Alp d'Huez.

When it was time to reveal the charade, Lance sent a team-mate to the front to push the pace on the lower slopes of the climb. Then came one of the defining moments of Lance's career: The Lookback. Alp d'Huez is steepest in the first 3 kilometers, and Lance chose the hardest section of the climb to attack. He rose from the saddle and danced on the pedals for a few seconds, then looked over his shoulder, right into his primary rival, Jan Ullrich's eyes to see if he could match him. The answer was no, and Lance exploded off the front for a convincing stage win. Throughout his Tour de France reign, Lance maintained his position as the race's most feared climber by concentrating on three things.

★ Increasing his aerobic capacity

★ Increasing his strength-to-weight ratio
  (also called power)

★ Refining his climbing technique

What Would
LANCE Do?

All hills are not created equal. And no one knows that better than me. From the rolling hills around my hometown of Austin, Texas, to the imposing Alps and Pyrenees of the Tour de France, I know the range of efforts required to conquer roads that go up.

Sprinter hills. This is my term for short, steep hills that take about a minute to go up and over. When I hit them, I usually get out of the saddle and power up and over the top. If there is a series of them, however, I'll stay in the saddle.

I have a specific workout for sprinter hills. I do it on a hill that takes about 30 seconds to ride in the highest gear that is comfortable (optimum gear). Each set in the workout consists of three repetitions. The first rep is in the optimum gear, the second in a higher gear so I feel slightly overgeared. In the third rep, I use an even higher gear—but not one so overwhelming that I can't get up the hill. I follow each set with 5 to 10 minutes of easy riding in a low gear over level or gently undulating landscape to recover before doing more sets. My sprinter hill workout usually consists of five or six sets.

Because this workout is intense, make sure you've warmed up with at least 20 to 30 minutes of moderate riding.

Rollers. These are hills up to 2 miles long. I stay in low gears, maintain a high pedal cadence, and remain seated for much of the climb.

Mountains. Again, low gears are the order of the day. I concentrate on pacing myself so as not to go anaerobic. I stand occasionally to bring different muscle groups into play, but I do so sparingly to avoid squandering my energy.

Aerobic Capacity

If you ride aerobically, theoretically you can maintain a steady pace indefinitely, assuming you eat and drink enough to stay properly fueled. In this state, your muscles absorb all the oxygen they need, and your body efficiently disposes of the lactic acid that your muscles produce as a byproduct of contracting.

When you exceed your aerobic, or lactate, threshold, your muscles strain, plunge into oxygen debt (anaerobic), and accumulate lactic acid. Crossing into this state is marked by burning muscles, side stitches, and shortness of breath. Your lactate threshold determines your endurance performance level because lactic acid shuts down the mechanisms that make muscles contract. To increase your lactate threshold for climbs, try this workout crafted by Chris.

ClimbingRepeats™
Goal: Increase your climbing lactate threshold
Where: A road with a long steady climb
How: Focus on continuous riding without interruptions for the length of the prescribed interval. Riding intensity should be in the 78 percent to 83 percent range of your maximum heart rate. Pedal cadence should be 70 to 85 rpm. Maintaining your heart rate intensity is more important than pedal cadence, however. The length of the workout should range from 5 to 15 minutes and recovery time between repeats should be 5 to 10 minutes.

Sample Workout
★ Total ride time: 75 minutes at 65 to 70 percent of maximum heart rate

★ Perform two intervals of 12 minutes each at 78 to 83 percent of your maximum heart rate.

★ Recover for 10 minutes between efforts.

Power
When Lance made the jump from triathlons to cycling in 1989, he already possessed great aerobic capacity. He soon discovered, however, that this was not enough to climb hills with the best. In the spring of 1991, Chris took him as a member of the national team to compete in the Settimana Bergamasca, a 10-day race in

Listen to the **COACH**

If climbing isn't a strength of yours, avoid getting dropped by stronger climbers by moving to the front before the climb. As the hill progresses, keep riding at your own pace and ignore the stronger riders as they (inevitably) pass. You'll lose places, but you increase your chances of remaining with the group as it goes over the top. Doing so will eliminate the need to expend energy to catch up on the descent.

northern Italy's Bergamasca region. It featured top international amateur and professional riders. The race's route covered mountains in the Dolomites, Italy's branch of the Alps, but no major climbs such as the ones in the Tour de France.

Lance rode very well. He finished with the front pack every day and eventually took over as the leader. It was a big moment for Lance when he pulled on the leader's jersey—vibrant yellow on the top half and bright orange below.

Wearing the race leader's jersey, however, didn't help him in the climbs. Nor did his thick muscles, developed from his triathlon training. Lance couldn't stay with the top climbers up the long, hard climbs. The best climbers tend to have small bones, minimal upper-body muscle, and such lean torsos that their ribs show. They usually weigh less than 145 pounds, which was 30 pounds fewer than what Lance weighed at that time. In the mountains, he did well enough to limit the damage and maintain his jersey. Lance ended up winning the Settimana Bergamasca, but he realized that to fulfill his potential, he had to improve his climbing.

Chris shifted Lance's training program to help him lose weight and improve his strength-to-weight ratio. Lance also began to use an SRM (Schoberer Resistance Measurement) meter that measured the watts he produced from pedaling. He and Chris measured the total wattage that Lance produced during a 30-minute workout. Chris divided that figure by Lance's body weight, measured in kilograms, to determine Lance's watts per kilogram at race or time trial pace threshold. This gave them an accurate strength-to-weight ratio figure.

Lance shed weight during his cancer treatment as the chemotherapy caused nausea. He went from 171 pounds to 158 pounds on his 5-foot 10-inch frame. As he resumed training to make his comeback, he regained his strength level and aerobic capacity without gaining back the weight. He returned to professional cycling lighter than before and with an improved strength-to-weight ratio. Here are two workouts that Chris designed for Lance's comeback.

HillSprints™
Goal: Increase power for uphill accelerations
Where: A flat road leading into a steep uphill
How: Roll along at a moderate speed (15 to 20 mph, depending on your stage of development) in a moderate to light gear. As you hit the hill, jump out of the saddle, stomping on the pedals as hard as possible. The resistance will increase as you head up the hill. You must stay out of the saddle for the entire sprint, which will increase the stress on your lower back, butt muscles, and triceps. Focus on holding this top speed for the entire length of the interval. These sprints should be 8 to 12 seconds in length, and full recovery between sprints is very important to allow for muscle rebuilding and to ensure a quality sprint workout. Normally, 10 to 20 minutes allows for enough recovery before adding another sprint to your workout.

Listen to
the COACH

To simulate a climbing position when exercising indoors, set the front-wheel stand on a telephone directory or dictionary. The elevated front wheel mimics the raised triangle that a rider's body assumes when going uphill. The angle engages hill-climbing muscles of the lower back, butt, calves, and triceps.

Sample Workout

★ Total ride time: 45 minutes at 65 to 70 percent
of maximum heart rate

★ Perform three HillSprints of 8 to 12 seconds each
at maximum effort.

★ Allow full recovery between efforts.

HillAccelerations™

Goal: Build power and climbing speed at your lactate
threshold

Where: A long, moderate climb, or on a trainer with the front
wheel raised 4 to 6 inches above the horizontal plane to simulate
your climbing position

How: Begin the climb slowly. When you reach the last 500
yards of the climb, gradually increase your speed. Time it so that
you are nearly at your maximum heart rate during the last few
yards of the hill. Then attack out of the saddle with a maximum
but controlled effort.

Sample Workout

★ Total ride time: 120 minutes at 65 to 70 percent
of maximum heart rate

★ Perform two HillAccelerations.

★ Allow complete recovery between efforts.

Climbing Technique

By early 1999, Lance had world-class aerobic capacity and
strength-to-weight ratio. But to become one of the world's best
climbers, he had to do one more thing: change his climbing style.

Prior to the 1999 Tour, Lance frequently rose off his saddle to
use his body weight to push down the pedals. On a 2-minute climb,
he typically stood up two or three times. There are distinct reasons
for getting out of the saddle on a climb, such as to climb a steep grade,
to accelerate to close a gap, or to bring different muscles into play.

Listen to
the COACH

As you crest a climb to within striking distance of the top, shift up one more gear. This will help to add more speed as you roll over the top and begin your descent.

Rising out of the saddle, however, uses more muscles that in turn increase oxygen consumption and boost the heart rate—all of which consumes more energy. In a major race like the Tour de France, with 3 weeks of relentless racing, Lance couldn't afford to waste energy.

Lance changed his climbing style by shifting down to smaller gears to break up the workload and by sitting longer in the saddle to conserve energy. To prepare for the 1999 Tour de France, he and the U.S. Postal Service Pro Cycling Team devoted a weeklong training camp to pedaling up the Tour's roads in the Alps and another week of training up the Tour's roads in the Pyrenees. Team Director Johan Bruyneel, himself a veteran of several Tours, followed in the team car. Lance and his teammates wore ear receivers so that Bruyneel could communicate with them on the team radio. Each time Lance rose out of the saddle, Bruyneel asked, "What are you doing?" Lance promptly sat back down and shifted into a smaller gear. By the end of the two training camps, he had changed his style to smaller gears and staying longer in the saddle.

Lance became a great climber by doing more than staying in the saddle longer. You can easily incorporate these other tips into your riding.

Breathe out. Many riders tend to take short, shallow breaths as more effort is needed. Instead of concentrating on sucking in air like those riders, Lance focuses on breathing out through his mouth and nose. This allows the lungs to expand naturally and helps him pull air back in. By concentrating on breathing deeply and regularly, Lance lowers his heart rate a few beats while keeping the same speed.

Lance climbing during Stage 9 of the 1999 Tour de France. To conserve energy, Lance stays seated in the saddle for 80 to 90 percent of his climbing.

Position yourself in the saddle. Lance stays seated for 80 to 90 percent of his climbing, so a proper position to maximize comfort and power is essential. Sit comfortably on the saddle and place your hands on top of the handlebar, next to the stem. Pull on the handlebar lightly, but make sure to keep your arms and upper body relaxed. Don't squeeze the handlebar.

As you start to breathe deeply from the climbing effort, slide your hands out to the bend in the bar. This opens your chest cavity to expand the diaphragm and ease breathing. Also, this position allows the angle of your hips to make greater use of the muscles of the lower back, butt, hamstrings, calves, and triceps. Lance doesn't climb with his hands on the drops because this tightens the angle of the hips and restricts his breathing.

Rise with power. When rising out of the saddle to pedal uphill, move your body over the bicycle to put weight directly over the pedal downstroke. Place your hands on the brake hoods and avoid rocking the bike back and forth in a pendulum motion because that adds tire resistance on the ground and decreases the bicycle's stability. Shift up one gear to avoid spinning too quickly as more power bears down on the pedals.

The Payoff

One of Lance's field tests to measure his climbing improvement was an arduous 12-kilometer climb (7.5 miles) that the French call Col de Madrone, nestled in the hills outside of Nice, where he has a second home. The old narrow road up the Col de Madrone twists and turns with varying pitches as steep as 12 percent.

The course record was set in the early 1990s by Swiss ace Tony Rominger, renowned for winning the Tour de France's King of the Mountains jersey. Before Rominger retired, he raced up the Col de Madrone in 31 minutes, 30 seconds.

In late September 1998, Lance rode it in 33 minutes, 47 seconds. Two weeks later, he went to the World Championship Road Race in Valkenburg, Holland, and placed fourth. In April 1999, he rode the Col de Madrone in 32:30. Two weeks later at the 160-mile Amstel Gold World Cup Race in Holland, he finished second—a tire's width from victory. Five days before the 1999 Tour de France, Lance rode up the Col de Madrone in 30:47. Chris told him that nobody would be able to stay on his wheel during the Tour's mountain climbs.

When Lance rode impressively during the 1999 Tour in the Alps and the Pyrenees, starting with a stunning win in the Stage 9 mountaintop finish at Sestriere, his performance looked like a breakthrough. Everyone commented on his new style of staying in the saddle and using smaller gears. But Lance had been working on his climbing for years. It just took several years for his hard work to pay off.

20

Descending

Lance's breakthrough into world-class descending came years before his 1999 Tour de France victory. It took place in the spring of 1991 in northern Italy's 10-day pro-am Settimana Bergamasca. Lance rode as a member of the USCF national team that included Bobby Julich, who went on to finish third in the 1998 Tour de France.

On the next to last day of the race, Lance wore the race leader's yellow-and-orange jersey. The racers pedaled up a mountain pass in the Dolomites, Italy's branch of the Alps, where snow was falling at the summit. Lance's tires slipped on wet pavement, and he crashed. His chief rival, a pro from Italy riding in second place overall, saw an opportunity to overtake Lance and charged down the mountain toward the finish, 12 miles away.

Lance, bruised and cut, got back up and remounted his bicycle. Down the descents, he cut the tangents tightly, rose slightly out of the saddle to keep his body upright over the road, and leaned his bicycle down, forcing the tires into the pavement. As soon as he whipped out of the curves, he put his bicycle upright. The more speed he carried out of curves, the less work he needed to get back up to speed. Lance not only succeeded in catching his rival before the finish, he also retained his hold on the leader's jersey.

Lance's dramatic ride in the Dolomites illustrates many of the basics of descending. Here's how you can add Lance's techniques to your bag of tricks.

Listen to
the COACH

Having your bicycle vibrate during a high-speed descent can be un-nerving. The causes range from an improperly aligned front fork to a frame that is out of alignment. Such a "shimmy" or "speed wobble" can be controlled by doing three things. First, hold the pedals parallel to the ground and clamp the top tube between both knees to give the bicycle more stability. Second, use both brakes together to reduce speed. Fi-nally, avoid any jerky movements that may add to the frame's wobble. Once you're back home, take your bicycle to a shop and have a profes-sional check out the cause.

Keep spinning. You'll rarely see pros coast down hills without pedaling. Spinning lightly, even when unnecessary, stimulates cir-culation in leg muscles, helps clear lactic acid built up during the climb, and keeps leg muscles warm.

Take a cue from the wind. When a gust of wind, a short up-hill, or a level stretch slows Lance's speed during an overall de-scent, he'll take the opportunity to pedal six to eight rapid strokes to maintain his speed. When the descent resumes, so does his easy pedaling.

Increase the effort. Shift to higher gears as needed to avoid wasting energy from overspinning. But take care not to ride a gear so big that your legs get bogged down on a flat stretch or a short uphill section. When Lance rides in the hilly country around his hometown of Austin, Texas, he frequently shifts up and down as the long descents occasionally rise into slight uphills.

Stay alert. With the higher speeds of descents comes less re-action time if trouble pops up. Watch for traffic from side streets and driveways (especially around blind curves that are unfamiliar), and debris in the road.

Choose your position. The classic aerodynamic position fea-tures hands hooked on the drops for maximum steering control and access to the brakes, back low to the frame, and butt pushed to the rear of the saddle to distribute weight over the length of the bicycle.

While this position is fine and does offer the most control, most riders don't need a highly streamlined position. It's more comfortable to rest your hands on the brake hoods, which still gives you a convenient reach to the brakes and allows you to see ahead and catch air to shave speed.

Keep your head perpendicular and look down the road as far as possible to anticipate braking needs. Bend your elbows to absorb shocks.

Absorb the conditions. To weather bumpy roads and allow your legs to absorb vibrations, keep the crankarms horizontal and hover slightly over the saddle. Use your knees to grip the top tube and stabilize the bike if you suddenly hit a pothole or debris.

Brake like a pro. To blunt speed without brakes, lift your chest so that it catches the wind.

If braking is necessary, feather both brakes to shave speed, particularly on long descents. On hot days, with a bright sun

What Would
LANCE Do?

While most of what I do can be adopted to improve your cycling, there are two instances when you do not want to be like me.

- To slice through the wind more effectively when barreling down Alpine descents at 60 mph, I move my hands close to the top of the handlebar, next to the stem. Not only do you lose stability if you hit a bump in the road, but your hands will be too far from the brakes to effectively react to sudden dangers such as traffic or curves.

- My fellow pros and I routinely stay bunched together on descents. For safety and maneuverability, add a bike length of separation from the cyclist in front of you for every 5 mph you're traveling.

Listen to the COACH

Never lean forward over the front wheel. If you hit a hole or debris in the road, you're a goner. Instead, move your body back so that your buttocks extend slightly over the back of your saddle. Also, avoid radical aerodynamic tucks with your stomach on the saddle and your butt hanging off the back. This technique, while common among mountain bikers, results in an unstable bike and loss of control.

heating the blacktop, coupled with extremely long descents such as in the mountains, braking risks overheating brake pads or rims. A worst-case scenario happened to Chris during the 1986 Tour de France. In torrid heat in the Pyrenees separating France and Spain, Chris's wheel rims heated up from braking at 60 mph down twisting, narrow roads. His rims grew so hot that the glue of his tubular tires softened, which reduced the tires' bonding to the rim. When he finished the stage, Chris noticed that the front and rear tire valves, which had pointed straight at the hubs when the stage began in the morning, had become cockeyed.

Brake in advance of turns. Begin braking before entering a curve because braking causes the bicycle to track straight and stay upright. Lean or lift slightly off the saddle and lean the bicycle by laying it down as needed. (For more information, see Cornering on page 176.)

Like many skills in cycling, descending around curves requires you to "read" the road. Down every hill that isn't arrow straight is a line that takes you on the tangent through every curve in the shortest distance. It is important to remember to use this technique only when you are absolutely sure that there is no traffic around the corner. No matter how tempting it may seem to cut across the middle on a winding country road, you shouldn't jeopardize your safety.

Even though Lance learned to race downhill very fast, he

Lance is perfectly positioned for descending during Stage 13 of the 1999 Tour de France.

didn't always stay on the road. Lance's abilities to "read" the terrain were put to the test during the 2003 Tour de France when the heat of the July sun melted the tar on the road to Gap. Spanish rival Joseba Beloki crashed heavily right in front of Lance, whose only choice was to shoot across a small patch of dirt that formed a bridge over a deep ditch. Had he missed that patch of dirt or not seen it, he would have probably joined Beloki in the hospital. Instead, he maneuvered his way downhill through a grassy field, dismounted and jumped over a ditch at the bottom, and rejoined the same group of racers he'd been with before his detour.

21

Sprinting

Lance achieved success early in his career because of his sprinting skills, but once he started focusing on the Tour de France, everyone thought his days of contesting sprint finishes was over. Then, at the end of Stage 3 of the 2004 Tour of Georgia, Lance surprised sprint specialist Ivan Dominguez by edging him out in the sprint with a perfectly executed bike throw.

A huge crowd had swarmed into Rome, Georgia to catch a glimpse of Lance, the US Postal Service team, and many of the top pro riders in the world race the Tour of Georgia. Stage 3 finished with a hard set of circuits around town. Lance was staying near the front to keep himself out of trouble, but when he realized he was in position to contest the fast, downhill sprint for the stage win, he decided to go for it. Completely committed, he launched himself toward the finish line. In the final meters, the top three riders were dead even until Lance shoved his bicycle forward, fully extending his arms and legs, to win by inches. A few months later, he again decided to contest a fast sprint to the finish, this time to overtake Andreas Klöden en route to winning Stage 15 of the Tour de France.

Lance regained his sprinting power in the summer of 2004 because he incorporated specific workouts throughout the previous winter and spring to develop his ability to produce explosive power. But sprinting isn't just for racers. It comes into play for a wide variety of demands, such as accelerating to get through a traffic light before it turns red, fleeing an aggressive dog, or keeping up with a group. Knowing how to sprint can save your life and can add enjoyment to your cycling. It helps you improve your coordination and agility for improved handling.

The Elements of Sprinting

Working with Chris, Lance started to develop his sprint in 1991. To this day, he still works on these skills. Sprinting consists of four elements.

1. Explosive power for fast acceleration. If you lack explosive power, you'll eat a lot of dust as others zoom by.

2. Top-end speed, which is the measure of the highest attainable speed during a sprint. A fast top-end speed keeps opponents at bay when they try to come around during the last yards of a race. A high top-end speed, however, does not guarantee sprinting success.

3. High pedal cadence.

4. Overspeed, which is a higher speed than what you typically ride, such as when you sprint downhill.

Most races in the United States require less top-end speed than those in Europe. Rather, American races demand more explosive power and quickness. A U.S. racer's competitive diet consists chiefly of criteriums—circuit races, typically in downtowns or industrial parks, of 50 miles or less, most often around a course that is 1 mile or shorter and features sharp corners. In these events, riders brake into the turns, then surge out of them, lap after lap. By the time the finish line approaches, the constant slowing and surging has worn down the riders so that their top-end speeds are reduced. Often, the first person out of the last corner crosses the finish line as the winner.

In Europe, road races typically run 120 to 160 miles, and the finishes hit higher speeds than American races. Typically, from 20 to 30 miles from the finish, the teams drive up the peloton's pace

The Need for a Solid Foundation

Depending on your age, level of fitness, and the time you have available to train, you should pedal 5 to 10 weeks to build a basic fitness foundation before stressing the muscles with sprints. Certain muscle fibers, such as calf and stomach muscles, contract repeatedly without much fatigue. They are called slow-twitch fibers, and they have a high aerobic capacity and can produce energy for extended amounts of time. Fast-twitch fibers produce energy anaerobically for sprint or power work. Most people have muscle-fiber composition that is 40 to 50 percent slow-twitch and 50 to 60 percent fast-twitch. Putting in a foundation of base miles conditions slow-twitch and fast-twitch muscle fibers. Foundation miles are done at a comfortable pace. Pedal speed should range from 70 to 95 rpm.

to discourage breakaway attempts and to set up their designated sprinters. It is not uncommon for the peloton to hit speeds of more than 40 mph in the final mile—and everyone is still waiting to sprint. Racing in Europe requires great stamina to remain a contender over 6 hours of competition, and then it requires a high-speed kick at the end.

By developing the four elements of sprinting, Lance was successful on both sides of the Atlantic. In the 2004 Tour de France, after more than 6 hours of racing in the mountains, Lance entered the final kilometer of Stage 17 in a group of five racers. With about 700 meters to go, German Andreas Klöden surged toward the finish line. It looked like had the win in hand, until Lance started to sprint from behind. Firmly in control of the overall race and with the yellow jersey secure on his back, he didn't need the stage win, but he had decided there would be no gifts in the 2004 Tour. He was there to contest every minute of every stage, and he quickly closed the distance between him sprinted past a very surprised Klöden just meters from the line.

The Mechanics of Speed Bursts

Sprints are short in duration, usually lasting about 10 seconds, or 200 yards. Pure sprinters, who compete in match sprints of two riders against one another on a track, cover 1 kilometer but are only officially timed for the final 200 meters. Here's how you can maximize your sprinting power.

Set up for the explosion. Choose a slightly higher gear than the one you can roll along in comfortably. Grasp the handlebar firmly on the drops.

Jump up. Start your sprint by coming off the saddle as your pedal goes past the 12 o'clock position. It doesn't matter which foot you start with, though it will probably feel most natural to start with your strong foot.

Increase pedal resistance. Shift as soon as you feel minimal pedal resistance. If you find you have to shift within the first 5 seconds of your sprint, you've lost momentum too soon and should have started your sprint in a higher gear.

The timing of shifts depends on terrain and wind conditions. If you're starting your sprint downhill or with a strong tailwind, you won't have to wait 5 seconds. Experiment with accelerations by using different gears for varying terrain and wind conditions.

Jumping up off the saddle gave Lance a needed burst of speed in the 1998 World Championships in Mondial, Holland. Here, he shows a classic sprinter's form: out of the saddle with hands on the drops.

Lance throwing the bike at the finish for those few extra inches during the 1998 World Championships.

Give it your all. Pull strongly with the arm that's on the same side as the pushing foot, counteracting your leg's downward force. Keep both arms fairly rigid so that the bike stays upright under you.

Maintain the right position. At first, keep your weight back so that the rear wheel gets good traction during the early, high-torque phase. Hold your body square to the bike. Let your hips and shoulders work in unison.

Settle in. As you pick up speed, relax. Alternately pull and release the handlebar in sync with your downstrokes. Slowly rotate forward, with your weight directly over the pedals, keeping your body fairly low for better aerodynamics. Don't let your legs straighten completely at the bottom of each stroke. You want constant, fluid power going to the pedals.

Look up. Keep your head as low as you can while still seeing where you're going. Many cyclists tend to get tunnel vision when sprinting.

Sit down. When you've reached your peak speed, sit back in the saddle and concentrate on getting as high a pedal cadence as possible.

Let the air out. Sprints usually last about 10 seconds, so breathing technique is not an issue. Lance exhales when he first starts his sprint.

Sprint Workouts

Developing a sprint is a year-round process. Rotate between each of these workouts to improve weaknesses or incorporate variety into your training. Adding one or two sprint sessions weekly is all you need. Select a flat stretch of road with little traffic and no intersections for at least a quarter-mile so you can sprint without distractions.

PowerStart™

Goal: Increase muscular power to the pedals

How: To begin, roll at a very low speed in a high gear, almost at a near standstill. Then, jump out of the saddle, pushing down on the pedals as hard as possible in a maximum effort. Pull on the handlebar for leverage, tilting the bike slightly back and forth to position your body over each pedal as you drive it downward. This is an anaerobic workout, and your heart rate will not have time to fully respond. Do this workout for 3 weeks, then stop for 2 months to allow your body to adapt to the stress.

Listen to the COACH

Sprint training is different from interval training. Sprint training requires full recovery between sprints—typically 5 to 20 minutes, depending on your fitness. This contrasts with interval training, which involves a series of sprints broken up with short recovery periods. Sprint training develops greater speed. Interval training stresses the body to make it adapt to greater physical efforts.

Training Zones

Ranges	% MSHR	% FT Average Power	Description
1	50–70	30–50	Easy riding, recovery training
2	50–91	45–73	Endurance base training
3	88–90	81–85	Aerobic capacity training
4	92–94	85–90	Lactate threshold training
5	94+	90+	Maximum aerobic training, increasing max VO$_2$

Sample Workout

★ Total ride time: 60 minutes in Zone 2

★ Perform five PowerStarts of 10 to 12 seconds each at maximum effort.

★ Recover for 5 to 20 minutes between efforts.

HighSpeedPedal™

Goal: Improve your body position and pedaling stroke during high-speed spinning

How: Pick a relatively easy gear (your easiest, or "granny," gear is ideal). Begin by slowly working up your pedal speed, starting with 15 to 16 pedal revolutions per 10-second count (90 to 96 rpm). While staying in the saddle, increase your pedal speed. Keep your hips smooth, with no bouncing or rocking. Concentrate on pulling through the bottom of the pedal stroke and over the top.

Take 2 minutes to build your cadence to 18 to 20 pedal revolutions per 10-second count (108 to 120 rpm), where you'll stay for the designated time. (See the sample workout below.) Your heart rate will climb while doing this workout, but don't use it to judge your training intensity. It is important to maintain cadence—ride the entire length of the HighSpeedPedal workout with as few interruptions as possible. Lance does this workout during the off-season as he works on the fundamentals of his pedal stroke.

Sample Workout

★ Total ride time: 45 minutes in Zone 2

★ Perform 15 minutes of HighSpeedPedal on flat terrain in the middle of the ride.

SpeedIntervals™

Goal: Improve your lactate threshold and develop repeatability in your sprints

How: Gear choice should be moderate, but pedal cadence must be high (110+ rpm). Speed, power, and acceleration are the key elements, not heart rate.

This workout builds up high levels of thigh-burning lactic acid, training your body to tolerate and dissipate it more efficiently. If you have to, shift into a lighter gear to maintain the cadence, but don't let the intensity of the interval drop. Keeping your cadence up will train your body's adaptation to high-speed efforts. Spin easily to recover from each interval.

Caution: Speed training is very stressful on the body and must be performed with recovery in mind. During those weeks you perform speed intervals, reduce your overall training hours.

Sample Workout

★ Total ride time: 75 minutes in Zone 2

★ Perform eight intervals of 40 seconds each in Zone 5.

★ Recover for 45 seconds between efforts.

Sprints

Goal: Develop cycling speed and acceleration and improve the effectiveness of fast-twitch muscle fibers

How: These sprints are always performed at 100 percent maximum output. Roll along at a moderate speed (15 to 22 mph). Stand up out of the saddle, accelerating the entire time, and return to the saddle after a few seconds to focus on maintaining high pedal speed (about 110 rpm) in a smooth and efficient form (back and shoulders steady, no bouncing on the saddle) for a sprint of 8 to 10 seconds, or about 200 yards.

Allow 5 to 20 minutes of recovery before the next sprint. Do a total of three to six sprints. These are basic sprints that may be practiced year-round to spice up your rides.

Sample Workout

★ Total ride time: 75 minutes in Zone 2

★ Perform three or four Sprints of 8 to 10 seconds each at maximum effort.

★ Allow full recovery of 5 to 20 minutes between sprints.

HighSpeedSprints™

Goal: Increase your top-end speed and peak power

How: On a slight downhill, roll along in a large gear at a high speed—but not your top speed (20 to 30 mph, depending on your stage of development). Jump out of the saddle and accelerate. Upon reaching top speed, return to the saddle and focus on holding that speed for the entire length of the sprint interval. Maintain proper form and a high cadence (110+ rpm).

HighSpeedSprints last 8 to 12 seconds with full recovery between each to allow for rebuilding of the muscles and to ensure a quality sprint workout. Because this workout is performed slightly downhill at high speed and pedal cadence, the power demands will be high due to the aerodynamic drag associated with beginning sprints at high speed.

Sample Workout

★ Total ride time: 75 minutes in Zone 2

★ Perform five HighSpeedSprints of 8 to 12 seconds each at maximum effort.

★ Allow full recovery of 5 to 20 minutes between each effort.

OverSpeedSprints™

Goal: Increase your downhill sprint speed and develop the skills to handle your bike at high speeds

How: On a slight downhill that is 50 to 150 yards long, pedal up to a speed of 25 to 30 mph, then stand up from the saddle in a moderate gear and accelerate as hard as possible for the entire downhill. Shift gears as needed to keep going faster. When the road levels off, drop back to the saddle and keep your leg speed high. Sprint for 250 to 300 yards along the level stretch, maintaining top-end speed for the entire sprint.

Do these sprints one or two times a week, with two to four sprints per session. Allow full recovery of 5 to 20 minutes between sprints.

Sample Workout

★ Total ride time: 60 to 90 minutes

★ Perform two to four OverSpeedSprints of 6 to 10 seconds.

★ Allow full recovery of 5 to 20 minutes between sprints.

Tactics

As important as technique is to successful sprinting, tactics play just as big a role. Explode too early, and the pack will rush by you before the finish. Make your move too late, and you'll never catch the leader.

Identify the speediest. Know who the fastest sprinter is in your group and stick by him with as little effort as possible. You don't want to waste energy and be blown for the sprint.

Be aware of conditions. If it's uphill or windy, wait longer before you jump. Conversely, if you're moving downhill or have a tailwind, make your move sooner since the sprint will end much quicker.

At the 2004 Tour of Georgia, the sprint involved a downhill. Lance's surge for the line began about 150 to 200 yards from the finish line. At the 1993 Tour de France stage to Verdun, Lance rode in sixth position on a flat road when he made his move at 100 yards to win.

Keep them off you. When you take the lead sprinting against one or more cyclists, you can foil the riders drafting behind with a

Out of the saddle, Lance sprints out of a sharp corner during Stage 18 of the 1999 Tour de France.

double kick. If you're leading the sprint, hold some power in reserve. Check on your opponents by looking under your arms to see if the drafting cyclists are making their moves. When someone makes an effort to come around and get past, tap into that reserve for a second kick. To discourage drafting if you're the leader, move from side to side. You can also "trap" a drafter against the side of the road.

Be a follower. Drafting behind a leader has its benefits. Not only are you working less hard as you benefit from his work, but you can watch his reactions much more easily than he can see yours. When you're ready to make your move, wait for the leader to glance back. When he does, make your move on his other side. This misdirection is often enough to give you a critical edge as you race to the finish.

Practice tactics with friends. Training solo, you tend to work on fitness and technique. Sprinting with one or more partners allows you to test and refine your tactics.

22

Time Trialing

Long known as the test of truth among cyclists, time trialing is bicycle racing stripped to its essentials. Time trialing's purity comes down to how much power a rider can exert and sustain for the duration of the event, where everyone races individually over the same course against the clock. If you go out too fast, you'll blow up and lose more time than you'll gain. It's a matter of pacing, which takes experience. You want to finish with nothing left. If you can sprint at the end of a time trial, you didn't go hard enough. If you're looking to enter competitive cycling, time trials are a good place to start. They introduce you to performing under stress without the risks that come with riding closely in a tight pack.

A large part of Lance's success in the Tour de France can be attributed to his dominance in time trials. Over the course of his seven victories, he won 11 of 19 contests against the clock. From the beginning in 1999, Lance's rapid cadence set him apart from his rivals. The prevailing pedaling style for time trials was to grind along in massive gear, but Lance used a smaller gear and ticked his legs over at a cadence about 20 rpm faster than anyone else.

When Lance returned to cycling after cancer, he was 17 pounds lighter than he had been in 1990 (from 175 pounds down to 158). The high gears he pedaled in training, essentially the same as other elite riders, taxed his legs with a buildup of lactic acid that quickly brought on fatigue. He and Chris soon tried another approach.

Chris drew upon his experiences as a coach to cyclists with different body types. Pedaling high gears is easier for large or heavily muscled riders. Where it was advantageous for big riders like Jan Ullrich to muscle big gears, Lance was smaller and had to take advantage of his aerobic power because smaller or lightly muscled cyclists can't take the muscle strain of mashing big gears. But they can match or even better the speed attained by bigger cyclists by pedaling lower gears at a faster cadence. Pedaling faster, however, requires a higher aerobic capacity to meet the demands for more delivery of oxygen from the heart and lungs.

One of the only opportunities to see the differences between Armstrong and Ullrich's pedaling styles side-by-side occurred during the Stage 1 time trial in the 2005 Tour de France. The German started 1 minute ahead of Armstrong, riding low over his machine with his characteristic slow and steady cadence. Behind him the defending champion was tearing up the pavement and closing fast, using the high-cadence pedaling style he'd already used to win six yellow jerseys. With four kilometers to go in the 19-kilometer stage, Armstrong caught and passed the former Olympic and World Time Trial Champion! Yet, even though it was the only time Lance ever caught and passed Ullrich in a time trial, he couldn't add it to his list of stage victories. That honor, and the first yellow jersey of the 2005 Tour de France, went to Dave Zabriskie, a young American on Team CSC.

Spin Faster

In order to adapt your body to the increased effort of pedaling at a higher cadence, you must train for at least 4 weeks at that higher cadence. Signs of adaptation include regular breathing and legs that won't tire as quickly at the higher spin rate. Here's a tip about how to get there and also some tips to ride a faster time trial.

Pedal a lower gear. In the off-season, dedicated cyclists ride a fixed gear that has light resistance in order to train at a higher cadence. You can do the same thing on a bicycle equipped with a derailleur by selecting a low gear. Avoid the temptation of the big ring, however.

A Sense of the Enemy

To time trial well, Lance had to develop a sense of his opponent: the clock. Ordinarily, in a massed-start race, he had everyone in the peloton to stimulate him. In the time trial's individual race against the clock, where riders start at 1-minute intervals, Lance rode alone.

His remarkable 1999 Tour de France time trial performances began with preparations that started 6 years earlier. After he won the 1993 World Championship Road Race in Oslo, Norway, he flew to the U.S. Olympic Training Center (USOTC) in Colorado Springs, Colorado, to work with Chris for 3 days of intensive physiological and biomechanical tests. His goal was to go even faster, especially in time trials.

They tried different aerodynamic handlebars that put him in a more forward position with his elbows closer together, resembling a ski-tuck position to reduce wind resistance, and flattened his back over the bicycle frame. They also used a different frame that put his seat tube at a steeper angle (78 degrees, compared to his road frame's 72 degrees) and rotated his hips forward.

Lance's tests coincided with the USOTC's acquisition of a new bi-

Eliminate race day sluggishness. On the day before a race, include a couple of short, intense efforts of 3 to 5 minutes each. These will open the lungs to clear out lactic acid. Under no circumstance should you ride them so hard as to cause fatigue.

Warm up thoroughly. Ever notice how the first interval in a set is always the most painful? This is because of lactic acid buildup. Warming up before a time trial starts the process of clearing the lactic acid before the race. Spend an hour riding to warm up, including the last 40 minutes on a stationary trainer, if possible, to control the effort. Go to the start line with a light sweat going.

Start on your nondominant leg. Set the pedal of the your nondominant leg between the 10 and 11 o'clock positions for the first downstroke. Why not lead with the stronger leg? You'll start quicker if your strong leg comes around for the second stroke to help build momentum faster.

cycle instrument system made in Germany. The system, SRM (Schoberer Resistance Measurement), provides information, including cadence and power output, measured in watts. A handlebar unit gives the rider figures from data recorded by magnets attached to the crankarms and wheels and also from a heart rate monitor worn around the rider's chest.

Cycling physiologist Edmund Burke, Ph.D., and Jeffrey P. Broker, Ph.D., of the USOTC, took Lance to ride on the nearby outdoor cement velodrome. They scrutinized his pedaling mechanics and tested him with the SRM to see if different aerodynamic positions kept his watts measurement the same. Tests indicated that Lance's pedaling power worked best with cadences in the range of 80 to 85 rpm. His best cadence rose after he came back from cancer with a lighter body.

Lance left Colorado Springs for his home in Austin, Texas, with new data that helped him and Chris revise his training regimen. He trained over the winter, and the next season started to ride faster time trials. His improvements helped him win the Tour DuPont in 1995 and 1996, the last year it was held.

Look up. Look as far up the road as possible for three reasons. First, your line will be straight. Second, keeping your head up improves your sense of balance. Third, helmets are designed to slice through the wind when your face is forward.

Stay low. One of the keys to riding your fastest is to maintain a good aerodynamic position. If you need to stretch your back on an uphill, stand, but other than that, stay low.

Maintain your form when shattered. When you become fatigued near the end, keep your form as smooth as possible. Riding in a jerky manner will add seconds to your time. To practice, anytime you're out on a ride and start feeling weak, convert a bad feeling into a positive experience by imagining you're in your USA Cycling district time trial where you've blown up and need to maintain form so that you can save seconds at the end.

7 Weeks to a Faster Time Trial

A popular time trial distance, including USA Cycling district championships, is 40 kilometers (25 miles). With aero bars, a rider in good shape can cycle it in under an hour. If you want to ride 40 kilometers in under an hour, or otherwise lower your time, then you should train by breaking your goal pace down into smaller segments and train to this program.

Week 1. Begin with a time trial course of 5 kilometers (3.1 miles) where you can ride hard without traffic interference, such as a country road or a circuit in an industrial park. Ride that course for 5 kilometers at your goal race pace. This allows you to feel what that pace is like.

If you ride 5 or more days a week, do a 10-minute recovery ride with easy pedaling, then do a second interval at this level of

What Would LANCE Do?

An advanced technique that I include in my training is motorpace riding, in which I pedal behind a motorcycle. Riding in the draft of the motorcycle raises the workout speed to that of a race or greater. I perform this workout on level ground at an intensity that is below my lactate threshold, meaning I ride aerobically so that my heart and lungs supply adequate oxygen to my muscles.

When the terrain is rolling to hilly, then the training intensity increases under strain to maintain speed uphill and I cross my lactate threshold into anaerobic riding. Once over the top, I can recover on the descents. Even though I'm riding faster while motorpacing, I continue training just as intensely as in other workouts.

One major caution, however: Motorpacing is very hazardous. It requires a cyclist who is highly skilled at drafting and a highly skilled motorcycle driver. I do these workouts only on roads with light traffic, a minimum of intersecting roads, and excellent sight lines. You may enjoy similar benefits by pacing behind a tandem team.

intensity. Perform this workout twice a week. Try it relatively early in the week, then allow 2 to 3 days for recovery, meaning easy rides, and ride again later in the week.

If you ride 2 to 4 days a week, do a 20-minute recovery ride with easy pedaling, then do a second interval at this level of intensity. Perform this workout twice a week. Try it relatively early in the week, then allow 2 to 3 days for recovery, meaning easy rides, and ride again later in the week.

Week 2. Extend the same speed to 7.5 kilometers (4.7 miles), and do it twice during your workouts.

Week 3. Stretch the pace to 10 kilometers (6.2 miles). Do that twice during your workouts to cover half of the 40-kilometer race distance at target pace.

Week 4. Continue working out at the same speed and distance, but reduce the recovery interval from 10 minutes to 5 minutes if you ride 5 or more days a week; or from 20 minutes to 10 minutes if you ride 2 to 4 days a week.

Week 5. Depending on how you feel, you can eliminate the break and do 20 kilometers (12.5 miles) at goal pace. If you feel stressed, repeat Week 4, then move on to Week 5.

Week 6. Move up to 25 kilometers (15.6 miles) at target race pace.

Week 7. In the final week, decrease workout distance to 7.5 kilometers to be ready for race day. This progression will condition the rider's body and give his mind confidence to go faster and ride a strong race.

Special Equipment

Aerodynamic gear has exerted a greater influence on time trialing than any other event in the sport. Clearly, a rider with better and more advanced equipment has an edge over his opponents in this event. At the professional level, all the teams have access to the same equipment for a more even level of competition. But at lower levels of competition, the advantage goes to those who spend the money.

Wheels

Steve Hed, one of Lance's first sponsors when he was a teenage triathlete, is a pioneer in applying aerodynamics to making bicycle wheels. Hed describes aerodynamics as the study of how a solid body, such as a rider and his bicycle, move through the air surrounding it. Hed began designing and building aero wheels in his garage in White Bear Lake, a suburb of St. Paul, Minnesota. From his garage, he helped to create a new industry.

"Atmosphere is what makes a person go slow," Hed says. "The majority of resistance is trying to push your body and equipment through the air. At 20 mph, 80 percent of an average rider's physical output is used to overcome the effects of drag when he rides on the flats."

Hed designed a wheel with a rim 65 millimeters deep (a little more than 3 inches), compared to the standard 20 millimeters to 25 millimeters (less than 1 inch).

"When the rim increases in depth, it becomes stronger, so it can use fewer spokes," Hed observes. "That decreases wind resistance and makes the wheel lighter. There are also aero spokes. Instead of being round, they are flattened to the shape of airplane wings to require less energy to turn."

Hed took the deep rim all the way to make disk wheels. "The disadvantage of disk wheels is that they weigh more than a standard spoked wheel," he notes. "So in a race, you're hauling around more weight, about 100 grams more (approximately 4 ounces)." Disk wheels also catch the wind, which makes riding them difficult in blustery conditions.

Lance has found that what works best in time trials is a disk wheel made of carbon fiber on the rear and either a deep-dish wheel with 12 aero spokes (instead of the standard wheel's 32 round spokes) or an wheel with just three carbon blades on the front. This combination is available through most bicycle shops.

Helmet

Lance's original teardrop time trial helmets were designed exclusively for the Tour de France and other professional time trials

2005 Tour de France, Stage 20 (individual time trial).

in Europe. They weren't available for sale in the United States, explains Tom Larter, product manager at Giro Helmets, based in Santa Cruz, California. Larter designed Lance's helmet with John Cobb, Lance's aerodynamics advisor who runs Bicycle Sports, a shop in Shreveport, Louisiana.

"We didn't sell that teardrop helmet commercially," Larter says. "Its high-tech molded plastic thin walls were not intended to absorb any impact in case of a fall. Lance's time trial helmet is made purely for reducing wind resistance. In recent years, after professional racing mandated protective helmets for all events, Giro designed a new time trial helmet for Lance and made it available to the public.

One option to make a regular road helmet more slippery through the air is to stretch a smooth Lycra rain cover over it. The ride may be hotter, but you could shave some seconds.

Aero Bars

The best way to get aerodynamic is to equip your bicycle with aero bars. Available in a variety of styles, they all stretch riders in a more forward position to sit lower to the bicycle frame, with elbows and hands close together in a ski-tuck position so the hands split the air around the rider. Cobb, who has tested Lance and Greg LeMond as well as equipment in the wind tunnel at Texas A&M University in College Station, Texas, observes that adding aero bars is "the biggest single improvement" that a rider can make to reduce drag.

"A cyclist riding with his hands on the brake hoods produces about 8 pounds of drag when he goes through the air," explains Cobb. "When the same guy rides a bicycle fitted with aero bars, he has about 6 pounds of drag. As a comparison, a family van driving at 30 mph produces a drag force of 1,200 pounds."

Placing your hands close together, however, makes handling a bicycle difficult—a factor that makes aero bars illegal in road races, even for experienced pros like Lance. Aero bars are used exclusively in time trials. Most weekend amateur racers competing in time trials benefit by attaching inexpensive clip-on aero handlebars to their road handlebars. Cobb recommends positioning the aero bars so that your forearms point a few degrees up. Otherwise, he warns, "If your forearms slope down, it's like throwing away the aero bars."

Cobb worked during the 1990s with Lance at the Texas A&M wind tunnel to make his position as aerodynamic as possible. The wind tunnel is a tube-shaped chamber. At one end is a four-bladed propeller 12 feet in diameter from the Enola Gay B-29 bomber that churns the air with a roar appropriate to the 1,500-horsepower electric motor turning the blades. Thirty feet away, the cyclist sits on his bicycle, which is bolted to a steel structure.

"As the propeller turns, it pulls air across the rider," Cobb explains. "That flexes the steel mount the bicycle is bolted to, and the computers measure the flex to give numbers that can be interpreted for drag forces. They'll measure down to $1/100$ of a pound of drag."

Cobb and Lance worked together over the winter of 1998–1999 to design aero bars and the position that he would ride during the 1999 season. Lance's aero bars consist of two segments. The forward-facing bars, which are round and extend straight from the head of the frame, are standard among professional cyclists and dedicated time trialists for slipping through the air along road stretches that are flat and straight. The second segment consists of the crossbars. They flare out as wide as his road handlebar to enable him to better negotiate turns and change his position to pedal uphill. "The crossbars are elliptically shaped instead of round like the forward-facing bar," Cobb notes. "Elliptically shaped crossbars contribute to reducing drag about one-tenth of a pound. It all adds up."

In 1998, wind-tunnel tests showed that Lance's drag when he was riding his aero bars in the time trial position measured 5.8 pounds. His power output over 55 kilometers (34.3 miles), which is typical of the Tour de France time trial stages, averaged about 410 watts, Cobb said.

"We did a bunch of things to improve Lance's aerodynamics," Cobb says. "Since he arches his back more because of his fractured vertebrae, what we did was sacrifice a little aerodynamics with better equipment." They also refined his elbow width on the bicycle. "I kept raising his elbows and shoulders," Cobb says. "So he sat an inch and a half higher on the bike in 1999 than he did the year before. Raising his position opened his chest up more so he could breathe better. That helped him increase his wattage. We reduced his drag from 5.8 pounds to 5.6 pounds while raising his potential wattage output from about 410 watts to 450 watts. It's like adding horsepower to a car—raising a 175 HP motor to 190 HP. That meant Lance changed from his family van to a Mustang for performance."

By January 1999, they had reduced his drag to 5.2 pounds. "Now it was like he was driving a Corvette," Cobb says. After Lance won the Tour de France, they continued making more refinements over the following winter. For 2000, they trimmed his drag to 5.0 pounds. "Lance has raised his watts, and he's got a big dose of confidence. Now he's driving a Ferrari instead of a Corvette."

Hed observes that top riders such as Lance pay close attention to aerodynamics to gain every advantage they possibly can. "For the 1999 Tour de France time trials, Lance used as much aero technology as possible," Hed says. "I doubt there was another rider in the Tour who paid as much attention to aerodynamics as Lance did."

Lance continued to refine his aerodynamic position throughout the rest of his career, spending time each winter in the wind tunnel finding new ways to reduce drag.

Time Trial Bicycle

This type of cycle is built to put a rider in the most aerodynamic position, yet it is so highly specialized that it has a very limited appeal for other uses. Of the 25,000 to 30,000 miles a year that Lance rides in training and racing, he puts in a maximum of 2,000 miles on his time trial bicycle. The aerodynamic crouch makes for faster speed but doesn't allow much looking around. Most competitive riders entering their district time trial championship and one or two other local time trials may be better off converting an old but serviceable road frame to a time trial bicycle with aero equipment. Another alternative is to look for a used time trial bicycle.

If you don't have a time trial bicycle, you can modify your road or touring bicycle with an aerodynamic handlebar that clips onto your regular handlebar. It puts you in a forward position, flattens your back, and brings your arms together in a ski-tuck position, with your elbows resting on padded holders to reduce frontal resistance. Lower the handlebar closer to the frame crown. If you feel pressure on your crotch, tilt the nose of the saddle down. If the pressure continues, raise the handlebar. To keep the hip angle open, slide the saddle forward on the saddle rails.

This position may take some getting used to, so try it out on casual rides over familiar roads. As discussed in Riding Position on page 35, you're balancing an aerodynamic position with comfort. No matter how aerodynamic your position is, it must to be comfortable enough to hold from start to finish.

23

Lance in Action

Lance's unbelievable comeback from cancer to win the 1999 Tour de France vaulted him into the domain of the sport's legends, earning him a permanent spot in the cycling annals alongside countryman Greg LeMond, the first American ever to win the Tour. LeMond, too, staged a storybook comeback, nailing two of his three Tour de France victories after recovering from a shotgun blast in a hunting accident.

The history of the Tour holds many similar heroic tales. But often, the technical jargon of bicycle training—max VO_2, intervals, lactate threshold, glycogen depletion, and on and on—obscures the sheer drama and adrenaline rush of this century-old sport. Likewise, it's difficult for an ecstatic fan to imagine the endless hours of preparation that go into training for a race like the Tour de France, which lasted 3 weeks and 2,290 miles in 1999.

To help bridge this gap, Chris and cycling physiologist Ed Burke, Ph.D., analyzed Stage 9, the most exciting in the 1999 Tour, looking at the strategy of the stage and how vital training principles came into play.

The Role of Recovery

On Sunday, July 11, Lance won Stage 8, the first of two 1999 Tour time trials, riding the entire 35.1-mile course in 1 hour, 8 minutes, and 36 seconds. That night, the Tour riders flew to Geneva, Switzerland, and traveled in buses to the start of Stage 9 in Le Grand Bornand, a popular ski resort in the Savoy Alps.

217

The day after this all-out assault—where he spent more than an hour riding at 188 to 192 beats per minute (at least 10 beats above his lactate threshold of 178 bpm)—Lance and the rest of the peloton got an official day of rest. For the U.S. Postal Service team, that meant a 2-hour recovery ride at an easy pace, allowing their bodies to purge lactic acid and restore muscle glycogen for use as fuel in Stage 9 the following day.

The Tour organizers positioned two such recovery days at key times in the 3-week race, recognizing that even world-class athletes like Lance Armstrong need time to recharge their batteries for the battles to come. The next day's stage loomed particularly large on the horizon—the first mountain stage, where the peloton would enter the high peaks of the Alps.

Stage 9 wound nearly 133 miles through the Alps from Le Grand Bornand in France to Sestrière in Italy. The route traversed six major Alpine climbs, including the infamous Col du Galibier, at 8,678 feet the highest pass of the race and a traditional barrier to Tour riders since the early years of the race.

In a press conference on the rest day, Lance said that the stage didn't favor his strengths. Having already won two stages, he told reporters, his goal was simply to defend the yellow jersey in a relatively passive, methodical fashion, not worrying about winning the stage.

Fueling the Engine

What Lance referred to as a passive defense turned out to be a savvy, relentless attack that gave him a decisive victory—the first mountain stage win by an American since Andy Hampsten took l'Alpe d'Huez in 1992. How Lance did it would make him a legend.

The Tuesday morning began under an overcast sky that threatened to turn cold, wet, and nasty in the high passes. At the start, a huge crowd of vacationers filled the town to cheer the 176 starters. A party atmosphere prevailed. Mario Cipollini, the Italian sprinter who had made Tour history by winning four consecutive daily stages, arrived for the sign-in ceremony dressed in a Roman toga over his cycling clothes, striking poses for photographers.

The racers had already covered a fatiguing 920 miles in
9 days of racing. Lance faced additional pressure because he wore
the *maillot jaune*—yellow jersey—of race leader, which he had
taken from Estonia's Jaan Kirsipuu after winning the time trial. He
was also the subject of tremendous international media attention.
He was a marked man everywhere he turned. The more attention
he paid to fueling his engine, the less he'd have to worry about his
body becoming his own worst enemy.

Lance and his teammates burned 7,000 calories a day during
the Tour, compared to sedentary but healthy men who require less
than 2,500 daily calories. The body can store only 1,600 to 2,000
calories of muscle glycogen, so Lance and the other riders had
taken in as much fuel as they could, particularly carbohydrates and
protein, to supplement the fuel stored in their bodies.

Soon after the riders left the starting line, they made a relaxed
descent that kept the peloton bunched together. Though all riders
had enjoyed a large breakfast high in carbohydrates, they still took
advantage of the downhill to eat and drink. Lance and the others
carried two 21-ounce bottles—one filled with spring water, the
other with a prepared sports drink high in electrolytes and carbohydrates. They also carried food in their jersey pockets—small
sandwiches with turkey or cheese, an energy bar or two, sliced apples, raisins, figs, and bananas.

Protecting the Team Leaders

At nearly 10 miles into the stage came the day's first "hump"—
a 2-mile climb up 2,600-foot Col du Marais—a mere warmup for
the miles and mountains that lay ahead. Ride leaders like Lance,
Alex Zulle of Switzerland, Abraham Olano of Spain, and Richard
Virenque of France rolled up near the front of the peloton.

Their support riders took over the front to set the pace and
protect their team leaders by shielding them from the wind. Support riders pedaled at a tempo pace, allowing the leaders to ride at
about 75 percent of their maximum heart rates—an effort slightly
below their lactate thresholds. Though the leaders went up and

over the peak gracefully, several less fit riders dropped off from the back of the peloton.

After reaching the summit, riders made another descent through a lush valley with mountain streams and chalets nestled in the hills. The descent gave riders the opportunity to rest their legs and to eat and drink again. Approaching 25 miles came the second climb, the nearly 3,000-foot Col de Tamié.

Stronger riders with a greater aerobic capacity and a higher lactate threshold went to the front and forced a pace that made other riders who had crossed their individual lactate thresholds fall off the back. None of the aggressors were contenders for the overall win, however, so Lance and the other race leaders bided their time.

"Once riders are off the back, they're gone," explains Chris. "They can recover, but it may take 5 to 10 minutes at a much lower intensity to allow their bodies to metabolize the lactic acid. In the Tour, when you fall behind the peloton by a gap of 5 minutes, it's usually all over for you for that stage."

The Ups and Downs of Racing

After the descent, the road leveled off and speeds increased. At the town of Aiton, the speed spiked to maximum as sprinters like Mario Cipollini and Stuart O'Grady of Australia went all-out in the stage's first intrarace sprint competition. The winner of each sprint receives points that determine who wears the sprint leader's green jersey. O'Grady won this particular race-within-a-race, but Lance was unconcerned. He had bigger fish to fry.

After the sprint, the riders relaxed. They ate and drank the rest of the food and beverages they carried. In Saint-Jean-de-Maurienne, 61 miles and about 2½ hours into the stage, the peloton went through a feed zone. Riders stuck out their arms to pick up a musette bag—a small pouch with a long cloth handle meant to be hooked in midride and slung over the shoulder of the receiving rider. The musette bags contained more sandwiches, energy bars, fruit, and two full bottles. Lance, as team leader, received his food

Lance (*right foreground*) climbing in the rain during the pivotal Stage 9 of the 1999 Tour de France.

and beverages from Frankie Andreu, who rode support and picked up Lance's bag.

At 77 miles, about 3 hours into the ride and past the mid-point, the peloton approached the first major climb, the 4,700-foot Col du Télégraphe. A cold, heavy rain fell with gusting winds. Frankie Andreu rode at the front of a small group that included other U.S. Postal Service team members. Lance drafted in their slipstream. Andreu pulled for 6 miles, then sat up for George Hincapie to take over the lead for a couple of miles. Lance crossed the summit in 12th place.

Thinning the Herd in the Thin Air

Up to the Col du Télégraphe, the climbs hadn't been at high altitude, although each ascent lasted longer than the one before. Still, the number of real contenders had dwindled to about a dozen.

"Physiologically, riding at or close to lactate threshold really sucks your energy," says Chris. "Even if you eat and drink throughout the stage, the most you can take in is about 400 calories per hour in solid food and energy drinks. But you're burning 600 calories per hour, so you can't avoid going into an energy deficit."

From the Col du Télégraphe, Lance and his group rolled downhill a few miles, leaving the rain behind. A breakaway led by José Arrieta of Spain had managed to gain more than 6 minutes, but the weather would only get worse—and the next climb, a 9-mile ascent up the quadriceps-busting Col du Galibier, nearly a mile high, would shorten the lead even more.

Around them were deep valleys leading up to snowcapped Alpine peaks. Chilly air, a steep grade, and hairpin turns interrupted the climbers' rhythm, stringing out the peloton for several miles—a half-hour behind the leaders. Teammate Kevin Livingston pulled Lance in his slipstream for several miles and looked good to last the rest of the race. But fitness means little when fate takes a hand. At the summit, Livingston dropped out of contention when the rain jacket he had been handed for the descent tangled in his front wheel.

Lance and his group were just under 2 minutes behind Arrieta, the leader.

The Mind Game

Livingston's demise left Lance without the protection of any teammates in a lead group of eight other fierce competitors, including heavy hitters Alex Zulle and Richard Virenque. Lance's yellow jersey looked dull and dirty from tire spray. He later admitted he was chilly and tired, but he saw from the grim faces of the riders around him that they were also feeling intense emotional strain.

"Training is 90 percent physical and 10 percent mental," cycling physiologist Edmund Burke once observed. "Racing is 90 percent mental and 10 percent physical." Lance and the other leaders were very similar in terms of their fitness and talent. The climb up the Col du Galibier brought every aspect of their training into play: the energy consumed on the bike, the ability to withstand riding at or above lactate threshold, the ability to keep a poker face yet decipher the body language of the competition.

Lance (*right foreground*) puts the finishing touch on the race leaders near the end of Stage 9. This stage was the turning point for Lance in the 1999 Tour.

After the summit came a long, swift descent that led to the fifth mountain of the day, a 6.4-mile climb up to Col de Montgenèvre at 6,070 feet. Down the hill, the riders could eat and drink and get back some fuel. Arrieta, alone at the front, decided he'd had enough solo action and allowed Lance and the other stage leaders to catch him. But Arrieta's job was done. He had winnowed the field down to the hardy few, isolating Lance among a group of climbing specialists. And as a bonus for being the first over the top, Arrieta earned 20,000 francs, or about $3,000.

Leaden clouds hung low as a gusting headwind and icy rain confronted Lance's group up a steep 4.4-mile climb to Col Montgenèvre laced with hairpin turns. Down the other side, with just a half-hour to go, Ivan Gotti of Italy and Fernando Escartin of Spain took a big risk and broke away from Lance's group.

Perhaps a less motivated rider, starting the stage with more than a 2-minute advantage overall, would have settled for a respectable third- or fourth-place finish, knowing that his overall lead was intact. But Lance saw this as his moment to attack. After a brief solo effort, Lance joined Gotti and Escartin in the lead. Seeing his opportunity slipping away, Zulle charged after the three leaders and managed to bridge the gap—but French climber Virenque could not.

Just as Zulle joined the group, Lance pushed the throttle, delivering his final blow. "I realized that if I allowed Zulle to rest up after he rejoined my group, I could get beat," Lance later related. "So I decided to go as soon as he had come back to us." Zulle, who later admitted he thought his stage win was in the bag, looked as though he'd been slapped—he simply could not muscle his way up the mountain as fast as Lance.

When Lance's team car drove up beside him after he opened a gap, he smiled, looked to the driver and said, "How do you like them apples?"

The Twin Blades of Concentration and Technique

Assume for argument's sake that Lance has the same aerobic capacity as Zulle, Escartin, and Gotti. What takes place physiologically to determine the winner?

"When Lance is riding at 82 percent of his max VO_2 and he goes up to 87 percent, he's tilting into his lactate threshold," says Chris. "For the three others to stay with him, they have to go higher to make up the difference. When they do, they go anaerobic and cross their lactate threshold significantly. That causes their muscles to produce a tremendous amount of lactic acid. So the game becomes a matter of pain threshold—who has the mental strength to endure?"

Lance's better climbing technique came into play as well. Lance had changed his climbing style to ride more economically by remaining in the saddle to conserve his energy. The four leaders all rode at about 12 mph up the climb to Sestrière, but Lance rode smoothly—pedaling a light gear so that he had a rapid cadence, seated in the saddle, hands resting lightly on the handlebar. The other three stood up out of the saddle and pulled on the handlebar, moving their bodies in a pendulum motion from side to side, using more energy. That put greater demand on blood and oxygen. Lance was climbing like a mountain biker—sitting in the saddle to go the same speed with less output of effort.

Going for the Kill

Lance had been on the bike for more than 5½ hours, burning energy and getting dehydrated. Fatigue was setting in. Months of long training rides at high tempo rates also had conditioned his body to maximize his fat burning and minimize his carbohydrate usage at intensities slightly below lactate threshold. In addition, the amount of food and fluids that he had been taking in for the first 4 or 5 hours in addition to the fuel stored in his liver and muscles made a difference.

On the radio plug Lance wore in his right ear, he heard his team director, Johan Bruyneel, say that he'd opened a gap. Lance checked his pulse rate and stomped some more—content that, somehow, he wasn't at his maximum. As the grade lessened on the terraced climb, Lance shifted into his big chainring—daring the others to catch him. He rose briefly out of his saddle and attacked to widen the gap to 12 seconds. At the 5-kilometer (3.1 miles) sign, Lance led by 30 seconds.

With 2 miles to go, Lance was 34 seconds ahead of a desperately charging Zulle. By another two-thirds of a mile, Lance expanded his lead to 43 seconds. He looked invincible. But suddenly he felt his body strain. He realized he was running out of fuel. Zulle, his mouth open wide for air, standing on his pedals for every advantage, chased in all-out pursuit to limit the damage Lance was wreaking. He surged ahead of Gotti and Escartin, who rapidly lost ground to settle for third and fourth places.

When Lance crossed the finish line—still accelerating—he was 31 seconds ahead of Alex Zulle.

Amazingly, Lance was already giving interviews by the time

fifth-place Manuel Beltran of Spain crossed the finish line 2½ minutes later.

The Training Pays Off

Old Tour hands and journalists witnessing the finish and seeing it broadcast around the world expressed surprise at Lance's demonstration of power and tactics. He and Chris saw it as an earned reward for many months of hard training to improve his max VO_2, raise his aerobic efficiency for a greater lactate threshold, and ride more economically.

Lance was characteristically modest about his remarkable win over the best climbers in the sport. "Everybody was wondering how well I could do in the climbs," he said. "This was not a total answer. It just means my legs were strong today and I hope it will stay this way."

2005 Tour de France champion Lance Armstrong.

Lance and his children on the podium of his 2005, and final, Tour de France win.

Update 2006

Lance Armstrong nearly retired before he ever won the Tour de France. Back in 1998, after abruptly dropping out of the Paris–Nice stage race, he flew home to Texas with no intention of ever racing a bicycle again. He had fulfilled the promise he made during his October 8, 1996 press conference; he had beaten cancer and returned to professional cycling. Mission accomplished, game over, time to move on with life. But fortunately for cycling fans around the world, Lance decided he didn't want abandoning Paris–Nice on a cold and rainy afternoon to be the final note of his professional career. He rediscovered his deep love and respect for the sport of cycling and returned again to begin an unprecedented dominance of the world's greatest race, the Tour de France. Yet, after winning the race for the sixth time in 2004, his thoughts again turned to retirement.

The decision to retire or race again in 2005 was a difficult one for Lance. He had already become the only rider in Tour de France history to win the race six times. He was obligated to ride the race one more time, but considered skipping a year and focusing on other races, like the Tour of Italy and others that intrigued him, before returning to the Tour de France in 2006. It was January by the time he made the final decision to race the 2005 Tour de France, and February before he announced his intent to compete for a seventh straight Tour victory to the public. And then at the Tour of Georgia in April he would retire on the Champs Elysees at the conclusion of the 2005 Tour de France. Lance said he would retire whether he won or not, but that he was going to the Tour to win, not to just ride a farewell loop around France.

Doubts about his fitness persisted throughout the spring of 2005; he didn't win a single race prior to the start of the Tour de France, and even had lackluster performances in time trial tests like Stage 3 of the Tour of Georgia. Word on the street was that he was distracted, spending too much time in southern California, and not training with the same ferocity and dedication he had become his signature. Chris and others close to Lance knew differently. Lance did get a late start to his training, but he had something going for him that few people realized—this was his last Tour de France.

In previous years, there was always another Tour de France after the one he was currently preparing for, which meant Chris had to be more careful to bring Lance up to Tour de France condition gradually so he wasn't too mentally and physically exhausted to continue training for the following year. Without another event to train for, Chris could accelerate Lance's training to get him ready in less time, but the cost would be that he wouldn't be able to maintain that fitness as long as usual. Since Lance was retiring after the Tour, it was a cost Lance could afford to pay.

Lance proved he was ready when he caught and passed perennial adversary Jan Ullrich in the Stage 1 individual time trial, yet his performance wasn't enough to secure the first yellow jersey of the race. That went to his former teammate, Dave Zabriskie of Team CSC. The young man from Utah wore the jersey well during the next 3 days, until he crashed heavily just outside the final kilometer of the Stage 4 team time trial. Had he fallen within the final kilometer, he would have received the same time as his teammates. But since he fell before reaching the final 1,000 meters, he received an individual time and handed the yellow jersey over to Lance, whose Discovery Channel team won the team time trial for the third year in a row.

The race continued to be exciting all the way to the finish in Paris. Lance's rivals knew this wasn't their last chance to win the Tour de France, but it was their last chance to beat Lance Armstrong en route to victory, and they went on the offensive at every opportunity. Ivan Basso, Jan Ullrich, Alexander Vinokourov, Francisco Mancebo, Levi Leipheimer, and Floyd Landis all gave their best, but to no avail. Lance won the final individual time trial of his career and wore the yellow jersey for more than two thirds of the race. He finished his career with 83 days in the yellow jersey, second only to the greatest cyclist of all time, Eddy Merckx, and with a total of 22 Tour de France stage wins. Also, 2005 was a great year for Lance's teammates. First the team won their third consecutive team time trial. Later George Hincapie, the only man to be by Lance's side for all seven Tour victories, won the hardest stage of the entire race, the epic summit finish at Pla d'Adet in Stage 15. Days later, two-time Tour of Italy winner Paolo Savoldelli sprinted to victory in Stage 17.

True to his word, Lance retired from professional cycling on July 24, 2005, from atop the podium on the Champs Elysees. He left the sport on top, on his own terms, just the way he wanted to. And he left an indelible mark on the Tour de France and the sport of cycling, giving us many memorable Tour moments:

- 1999: Wins the prologue to surprise the world and take the yellow jersey. Storms past Abraham Alano en route to winning the Metz time trial. Shocks the climbing specialists by leaving them behind on the climb to Sestriere.

- 2000: Takes yellow jersey on the epic stage to Hautacam by catching and passing climbing aces Fernando Escartin, Richard Virenque, Marco Pantani, and Alex Zulle. Comes within 42 seconds of catching stage winner Xavier Oxtoa, who started the climb with an 8-minute advantage. Pantani wins stage atop Mont Ventoux, and uncertainty about whether the stage was won or given to Pantani starts a feud with Armstrong about "gifts."

- 2001: The Lookback. Lance feigns weakness on the Col du Glandon then launches a blistering attack at the base of Alp d'Huez, only after famously looking back over his shoulder to check on rival Jan Ullrich. Wins atop Alp d'Huez, and then wins the climbing time trial to Chamrousse the next day.

- 2002: The year of the Blue Train. Armstrong's superlative team explodes the peleton by setting a super-fast tempo on the climbs. Lance wins back to back stages to La Mongie and Plateau de Beille.

- 2003: Lance goes cyclocrossing through a field to avoid Joseba Beloki after the Spaniard crashed heavily on melted tar. Suffers dehydration crisis in the Stage 12 time trial and loses 1:36 to Jan Ullrich, who 2 days later comes within 15 seconds of taking the yellow jersey. Hooks a fan's mussette bag and crashes on the climb to Luz Ardiden; remounts and wins the stage to extend his lead to 1:07. Wins the final individual time trial in the rain, during which Ullrich crashes in a slick roundabout. Narrowest winning margin of his seven victories, at only 61 seconds.

- 2004: Becomes the only man to win the Tour six times. Wins 5 individual stages, 6 when you include the team time trial which the US Postal Service won for the second year in a row. Catches and passes Ivan Basso en route to victory in the Alp d'Huez mountain time trial. Sprints past Andreas Klöden to win Stage 17, in the spirit of "no gifts."

- 2005: Becomes the only man to win the Tour seven times, and retires on the Champs Elysees. Finishes career with 83 yellow jerseys, 22 stage wins, and records for the fastest ever team time trial and Tour de France average speed. Longtime teammate and friend George Hincapie wins the epic mountain stage atop Pla d'Adet.

There may someday be a cyclist who will challenge his record of seven Tour de France victories, but there will never again be a champion like Lance Armstrong. His comeback from cancer replaced the image of a cancer survivor as a fragile human being with the image of a champion with the potential to conquer the world, and his achievements have inspired millions in their fight against cancer. By 2006, the Lance Armstrong Foundation sold more than 55 million Livestrong bracelets and raised more than 13 million dollars for cancer research.

Photo Credits

Cover Photos by Graham Watson

Patrick Boutroux/Presse Sports: page 9
Courtesy of Chris Carmichael: pages vii, 39
Mel Lindstrom: pages 25, 34
Mitch Mandel/Rodale Images: pages 65, 68, 99–101, 105–112, 135
Doug Pensinger/Allsport: pages xvi, 155, 188, 194
Mike Powell/Allsport: page 4
Beth Schneider: pages 142, 205
James Startt: pages 42, 91, 152, 196, 197
Graham Watson: pages xvii, 1, 6, 18, 51, 131, 153, 163, 167, 175, 177, 180, 213, 223, 226, 227

Index

Boldface page references indicate photographs. <u>Underscored</u> references indicate boxed text.